M

MUSIC AND BOOKS ON MUSIC

Library of Congress Classification

1998 EDITION

Prepared by the
Cataloging Policy
and Support Office,
Library Services

Library of Congress, Cataloging Distribution Service, Washington, D.C.

The additions and changes in Class M adopted while this work was in press will be cumulated and printed in List 273 of *LC Classification—Additions and Changes*

Library of Congress Cataloging-in-Publication Data

Library of Congress.
Library of Congress classification. M. Music, books on music / prepared by the Cataloging Policy and Support Office, Library Services. — 1998 ed.
p. cm.
Includes index.
ISBN 0–8444–0981–2
—— ——— copy 3 Z663.78.C5M 1999
1. Classification, Library of Congress. 2. Classification—Books—Music. 3. Classification—Music. I. Library of Congress. Cataloging Policy and Support Office. II. Title. III. Title: Music, books on music.
Z696.U5M 1999
025.4'678—dc21 99–11719
CIP

For sale by the Cataloging Distribution Service, Library of Congress, Washington, DC 20541

PREFACE

Class M was created by Oscar G.T. Sonneck, first chief of the Music Division of the Library of Congress, and was one of the first schedules to be adopted in the new classification scheme the Library began developing late in the year 1900. The Music Division began to use Class M in 1902, and the first edition was published in 1904. A revised edition, also called the second edition, was published in 1917; it was reprinted twice with supplementary pages for additions and changes, first in 1957 and then in 1968. In 1978 the third edition was published as an integrated schedule that incorporated additions and changes made through June 1977. The present edition contains additions and changes made by the Library of Congress through September 1998. This is the first version of Class M to be published from a machine-readable database.

Apart from periods of intensive schedule development, new or revised numbers, captions, and index terms are added to the classification schedules as a result of proposals made by cataloging staff of the Library of Congress and cooperating institutions. Upon review and approval of these proposals in weekly editorial meetings of the Cataloging Policy and Support Office, the database is modified accordingly.

Conversion of the Library of Congress Classification to machine-readable form became possible with the provisional approval in 1990 of the *USMARC Format for Classification Data*. In 1992, the Library began to convert the schedules under the guidance of Rebecca Guenther, Network Development and MARC Standards Office. During 1993 and 1994, the Cataloging Distribution Service developed programs for producing printed classification schedules from MARC classification records in cooperation with Lawrence Buzard, editor of the classification schedules, Paul Weiss, senior cataloging policy specialist, and Rebecca Guenther. The Cataloging Distribution Service also coordinated the layout and design of the new schedules. Automation of schedule data and of publication allow for the production of new editions on a regular and frequent basis.

Class M was converted to the MARC format, edited, and indexed by Geraldine Ostrove, senior cataloging policy specialist for music, with the close collaboration of Harry Price, a music cataloger

INTRODUCTION

Conversion of the Library of Congress classification to online form has resulted in a Class M schedule that differs somewhat in appearance from previous editions. The process of conversion also provided an opportunity to revise the contents of the schedule in several ways.

Revisions include the Glossary and General Guidelines, tables at the end of the schedule, updated and standardized caption language, more notes and table references explaining the use of individual classes and spans of classes, recast footnotes as either explicit classification numbers or as tables for subarrangements, addition of captions to clarify hierarchies implied but not previously indicated, some new and revised class numbers, and a completely revised index.

Whereas the typeset and typed editions of Class M allowed certain number sequences to be expressed by ellipses that provided a compact visual presentation, in the 1998 edition those sections are fully explicit, represented as they appear in a shelflist. Finally, all references to the classed catalog were removed. That catalog, which the Library of Congress Music Division used instead of subject headings for form and topical access to musical works, was closed when the Library closed its card catalogs on January 1, 1981, at the time the *Anglo-American Cataloguing Rules*, second edition, was implemented.

GLOSSARY AND GENERAL GUIDELINES

References to the terms that follow are found in the Index, which leads users to the first classification number where the term applies, and from that class or range of classes to the explanation of the term in this list. It was not possible to refer from the Index, which is generated automatically from MARC classification records without manual intervention, directly to this Glossary, which is not part of the classification database.

Collection. Class as a **Collection** 1) an item containing compositions by two or more composers, 2) an item containing works by one composer and selected from two or more of the composer's works, or 3) an item containing one composer's works in more different forms or for a greater variety of performers than are provided for by any more specific class. Class as a **Miscellaneous collection** an item containing both original and arranged works. If the available classes for the medium of performance do not include Miscellaneous collections, class the item with Collections. Class as a **General collection** an item containing a greater variety of forms or types of works than may be provided for by any more specific neighboring class. Where expressly provided for in captions or notes under captions, class as a **Special collection** an item containing two or more works by one or more composers that are of the type indicated for separate works, e.g., class collections of string quartets as well as individual string quartets in M452-M452.4. See also Set.

Continuo. Class works with continuo parts as if the continuo were played by one, not two, performers, and, in general, as if the chordal portion of the continuo part were for piano (harpsichord, etc.); e.g., class a suite for violin and continuo consisting of harpsichord and violoncello in M220. If the chordal portion is for an instrument other than piano (harpsichord, etc.), assign the class that provides for the chordal instrument the work specifies; e.g., class a sonata for flute and continuo consisting of guitar and violoncello in M297.

Instructive edition. An edition of a work heavily annotated with textual instructions about how to practice and interpret various passages. Do not class as instructive editions those that merely contain standard interpretive markings, fingering, etc., whether the composer's own or subsequently added.

Manuscript. Class manuscripts of musical works in the hand of the composer or arranger in ML96. Class facsimiles and other reproductions of such manuscripts that are not meant as performance editions in ML96.5. Class with published musical works copyists' manuscripts and reproductions or facsimiles in any hand that are intended as performance editions.

Piano. Unless specific classes are otherwise available, the term is meant to include harpsichord, clavichord, virginal, and similar keyboard instruments whose strings are plucked or struck.

Piece. A musical work that does not fall into any available class for a specific form. The caption Pieces, when used for a span of numbers, may have subordinate classes for musical works in specific forms.

Score. Class with scores separate sets of parts and scores with parts.

Set. A group of compositions *published* as a single work. Examples are:

Three piano sonatas, op. 2, by Beethoven
Sieben Lieder, op. 48, by Brahms
Italienisches Liederbuch, by Hugo Wolf
Il quinto libro de madrigali, by Monteverdi

Studies and exercises. Class in MT studies and exercises, with or without accompaniment, that are pedagogical works. Class concert works titled studies by medium of performance in subclass M.

Teaching piece. A work composed principally for pedagogical purposes.

OUTLINE

MUSIC

M

LITERATURE ON MUSIC

ML

MUSICAL INSTRUCTION AND STUDY

MT

TABLES

INDEX

OUTLINE

M	1-5000	Music
	1.A1-1.A15	Music printed or copied in manuscript in the United States or the colonies before 1860
	1.A5-2.3	Collections
	2-2.3	Collections of musical sources
	3-3.3	Collected works of individual composers
	3.3	First editions
	5-1490	Instrumental music
	6-175.5	Solo instruments
	176	Instrumental music for motion pictures
	176.5	Instrumental music for radio and television
	177-990	Music for two or more solo instruments
	180-298.5	Duets
	300-386	Trios
	400-486	Quartets
	500-586	Quintets
	600-686	Sextets
	700-786	Septets
	800-886	Octets
	900-986	Nonets and larger combinations of purely chamber music
	990	Chamber music for instruments of the 18th century and earlier
	1000-1075	Orchestra
	1100-1160	String orchestra
	1200-1269	Band
	1270	Fife (bugle) and drum music, field music, etc.
	1350-1353	Reduced orchestra
	1356-1356.2	Dance orchestra and instrumental ensembles
	1360	Mandolin and similar orchestras of plucked instruments
	1362	Accordion band
	1363	Steel band
	1365	Minstrel music
	1366	Jazz ensembles
	1375-1420	Instrumental music for children
	1450	Dance music
	1470	Chance compositions
	1473	Electronic music
	1480	Music with color or light apparatus
	1490	Music printed before 1700 or copied in manuscript before 1700
	1495-5000	Vocal music
	1497-1998	Secular vocal music

OUTLINE

M		Music
		Vocal music
		Secular vocal music - Continued
	1500-1527.8	Dramatic music
	1528-1529.5	Duets, trios, etc., for solo voices
	1530-1546.5	Choruses with orchestra or other ensemble
	1547-1600	Choruses, part-songs, etc., with accompaniment of keyboard or other solo instrument, or unaccompanied
	1608	Choruses, etc., in tonic sol-fa notation
	1609	Unison choruses
	1610	Cantatas, choral symphonies, etc., for unaccompanied chorus (secular and sacred) with or without solo voices
	1611-1624.8	Songs
	1625-1626	Recitations with music
	1627-1853	National music
	1900-1978	Songs (part and solo) of special character
	1985	Musical games
	1990-1998	Secular music for children
	1999-2199	Sacred vocal music
	1999	Collections
	2000-2007	Oratorios
	2010-2017.6	Services
	2018-2019.5	Duets, trios, etc. for solo voices
	2020-2036	Choruses, cantatas, etc.
	2060-2101.5	Choruses, part-songs, etc., with accompaniment of keyboard or other solo instrument, or unaccompanied
	2102-2114.8	Songs
	2115-2146	Hymnals. Hymn collections
	2147-2188	Liturgy and ritual
	2147-2155.6	Roman Catholic Church
	2156-2160.87	Orthodox churches
	2161-2183	Protestant churches
	2184	Other Christian churches
	2186-2187	Jewish
	2188	Other non-Christian religions
	2190-2196	Sacred vocal music for children
	2198-2199	Gospel, revival, temperance, etc. songs
	5000	Unidentified compositions
ML	1-3930	Literature on music
	25-28	Societies and organizations
	32-33	Institutions
	35-38	Festivals. Congresses
	40-44	Programs

OUTLINE

ML		Literature on music - Continued
	47-54.8	Librettos. Scenarios
	62-90	Special aspects Including writings of musicians
	93-96.5	Manuscripts, autographs, etc.
	100-109	Dictionaries. Encyclopedias
	110-111.5	Music librarianship
	112-112.5	Music printing and publishing
	112.8-158.8	Bibliography
	113-118	International
	120	National
	132	Graded lists. By medium
	135	Manuscripts
	136-158	Catalogs. Discography
	158.4-158.6	Video recordings
	158.8	Computer software
	159-3775	History and criticism
	162-197	Special periods
	162-169	Ancient
	169.8-190	Medieval. Renaissance
	193-197	1601-
	198-360	By region or country
	198-239	America
	240-325	Europe
	330-345	Asia
	348	Arab countries
	350	Africa
	360	Australia, Oceania
	385-429	Biography
	430-455	Composition
	459-1380	Instruments and instrumental music
	465-471	By period
	475-547	By region or country
	475-486	America
	489-522	Europe
	525-541	Asia
	544	Africa
	547	Australia, Oceania
	548	Jews
	549-1093	Instruments
	549.8-649	Organ
	649.8-747	Piano, clavichord, harpsichord, etc.
	749.5-927	Bowed string instruments
	929-990	Wind instruments
	999-1015	Plucked instruments
	1030-1049	Percussion instruments
	1049.8-1091	Mechanical and other instruments

OUTLINE

ML		Literature on music
		History and criticism
		Instruments and instrumental music
		Instruments-Cont.
	1091.8-1093	Electronic instruments
	1100-1165	Chamber music
	1200-1270	Orchestra
	1299-1354	Band
	1379-1380	Electronic music. Computer music
	1400-3275	Vocal music
	1499-1554	Choral music
	1600-2881	Secular vocal music
	2900-3275	Sacred vocal music
	3300-3354	Program music
	3400-3465	Dance music
	3469-3541	Popular music
	3544-3775	National music
	3800-3923	Philosophy and physics of music
	3845-3877	Aesthetics
	3880-3915	Criticism
	3928-3930	Literature for children
MT	1-960	Musical instruction and study
	1-5	History and criticism
	5.5-7	Music theory
	20-32	Special methods
	40-67	Composition. Elements and techniques of music
	58-67	Forms
	68	Improvisation. Accompaniment. Transposition
	70-74	Instrumentation and orchestration
	73	Band
	90-146	Analysis and appreciation of musical works
	95-100	Opera, ballet, etc.
	110-115	Oratorios, cantatas, etc.
	125-130	Orchestral music
	140-145	Chamber and solo instrumental music
	146	Popular music
	170-810	Instrumental techniques
	180-198	Organ
	192	Electronic keyboard instruments
	200-208	Reed organ
	220-255	Piano
	259-338	String instruments
	260-279.7	Violin
	280-298	Viola
	300-318	Violoncello
	320-334	Double bass

OUTLINE

MT	Musical instruction and study
	Instrumental techniques - Continued
339-533	Wind instruments
340-359	Flute
360-379	Oboe
380-392	Clarinet (A, Bb, C, Eb, etc.)
400-415	Bassoon
418	Brass instruments
420-432	Horn
440-456	Trumpet
460-472	Trombone
480-488	Tuba
500-510	Saxophone
539-654	Plucked instruments
540-557	Harp
560-570	Banjo
580-599	Guitar
600-612	Mandolin
620-634	Zither
640-654	Lute, balalaika, etc.
655-725	Percussion and other instruments
728-728.3	Chamber music
730	Orchestra
733-733.6	Band
740-810	Instrumental techniques for children
820-915	Singing and vocal technique
825-850	Systems and methods
855-883	Special techniques
898-915	Techniques for children
918-948	School music
955-956	Musical theater

M

Music
For guidelines on classifying manuscripts, see Manuscript in the Glossary and General Guidelines following the Introduction
For guidelines on classifying a group of compositions published as a single work, see Set in the Glossary and General Guidelines following the Introduction
Music printed or copied in manuscript in the United States or the colonies before 1860
Early to 1820
1.A1 General
1.A11 Collections of sheet music bound into volumes by their original owners
1820-1860
Sheet music for copyright deposit
Contained in about 300 volumes arranged by district court and year
1.A12I Instrumental
1.A12V Vocal
1.A12Z Instrumental and vocal
1.A13 General
1.A15 Collections of sheet music bound into volumes by their original owners
Collections
Including music with literary matter
For a definition of Collection, see the Glossary and General Guidelines following the Introduction
1.A5-Z Miscellaneous
Class here collections of works by two or more composers for miscellaneous combinations of instruments and/or voices
For a definition of Miscellaneous collection see the Glossary and General Guidelines following the Introduction
For miscellaneous collections of works by one composer, see M3.1
Collections of musical sources
Class here historical publications, facsimile reprints, etc.
For collections of special types, see the appropriate classes below, e.g., M6, Organ music
2 General

Collections
Collections of musical sources -- Continued
2.1 Copyists' manuscripts
For guidelines on classifying manuscripts, see Manuscript in the Glossary and General Guidelines following the Introduction
For Catholic liturgical manuscripts (any year), see M2147
For copyists' manuscripts written in the United States before 1820, see M1.A1
For copyists' manuscripts written outside of the United States before 1700, see M1490
For Orthodox liturgical manuscripts (any year), see M2156
2.3.A-Z By region or country, A-Z
Collected works of individual composers
3 Complete editions
3.1 Selections
Class here collections of miscellaneous instrumental and/or vocal music by one composer
For collections for a specific or general medium, e.g., orchestra, piano, chorus (sacred or secular), instrumental ensemble, etc., see classes for the medium
3.3 First editions
Class here first editions by composers listed below. Class first editions by other composers by medium of performance or other appropriate class
J.S. Bach, W.F. Bach, Beethoven, Berlioz, Brahms, Chopin, Debussy, Dvořák, Fauré, Stephen Foster, Handel, J. Haydn, Kuhnau, Lanner, Liszt, C.F. Loewe, MacDowell, Mendelssohn, W.A. Mozart, Nevin, Puccini, Purcell, Schubert, Schumann, Scriabin, O.G.T. Sonneck, E. Strauss, Johann Strauss (1804-1849), Johann Strauss (1825-1899), Josef Strauss, Wagner, Weber
Instrumental music
5 Collections
Class here collections of works by two or more composers for miscellaneous combinations of instruments
For collections of miscellaneous instrumental works by one composer, see M3.1
Solo instruments
Organ
6 Miscellaneous collections
Original compositions
7 General collections
Special collections. Separate works
For a definition of Special collection, see the Glossary and General Guidelines following the Introduction
8 Sonatas

Instrumental music
Solo instruments
Organ
Orginal compositions
Special collections.
Separate works -- Continued

8.5 Symphonies
9 Suites. Variations
10 Fugues with or without preludes
11 Pieces
For a definition of Piece and the use of Pieces as a caption, see the Glossary and General Guidelines following the Introduction
Class here separate works only
11.2 Pedal pieces
Arrangements
12 Collections
13 Separate works
14 Organ books
Class here organ accompaniments to collections of psalms, hymns, etc.
14.3 Liturgical music
Class here works composed for liturgical purposes
For accompaniments, see M14
Special seasons and occasions
14.4.A-Z Collections. By season, occasion, etc., A-Z
For two seasons, etc., cutter for the first
14.4.A1 Three or more seasons, etc.
14.4.A4 Advent
14.4.C5 Christmas
14.4.E2 Easter
14.4.E6 Epiphany
14.4.F8 Funeral music
14.4.H2 Harvest. Thanksgiving
14.4.H5 Holy communion
14.4.H6 Holy Week
14.4.L5 Lent. Passiontide
14.4.P4 Palm Sunday
Passiontide, see M14.4.L5
Pentecost Festival, see M14.4.W4
Thanksgiving, see M14.4.H2
14.4.W3 Wedding music
14.4.W4 Whitsuntide. Pentecost Festival
14.5.A-Z Separate works. By season, occasion, etc., A-Z
For two seasons, etc., cutter for the first
14.5.A1 Three or more seasons, etc.
14.5.A4 Advent
14.5.C5 Christmas
14.5.E2 Easter
14.5.F8 Funeral music
14.5.H2 Harvest. Thanksgiving

Instrumental music
Solo instruments
Organ
Special seasons and occasions
Separate works. By season, occasion, etc., A-Z -- Continued
14.5.H5 Holy communion
14.5.H6 Holy Week
14.5.L5 Lent. Passiontide
14.5.P4 Palm Sunday
Passiontide, see M14.5.L5
Pentecost Festival, see M14.5.W4
Thanksgiving, see M14.5.H2
14.5.W3 Wedding music
14.5.W4 Whitsuntide. Pentecost Festival
Organ music for radio, see M1527.5+
Organ music for silent films and music not intended for specific motion pictures, see M176
Organ music for specific motion picture sound tracks, see M1527+
Organ music for television, see M1527.7+
Electronic organ
For special seasons and occasions, see M14.4+
14.8 Collections
14.85 Separate works
15-19 Reed organ (Table M2)
Piano
For a definition of Piano, see the Glossary and General Guidelines following the Introduction
For piano, three or more hands see M198-M213
20 Miscellaneous collections
Collections relating to the Civil War
Class here works published in the United States during the Civil War era that relate by title or otherwise to the Civil War
20.C58 General
20.C59 Union
20.C61 Confederate
20.E7 Collections relating to World War I
Original compositions
General collections
21 Two or more composers
22 One composer
Special collections. Separate works
23 Sonatas
24 Suites
25 Pieces
Class here separate works only
25.2 Double keyboard, Janko keyboard, etc.
25.3 Two pianos, one performer
Piano, 1 hand
26 Left hand
26.2 Right hand

Instrumental music
Solo instruments
Piano
Original compositions
Special collections.
Separate works -- Continued
27 Variations
28 Marches
Dances
30 General
31 Two-rhythm (polka, etc.)
32 Three-rhythm (waltz, etc.)
Arrangements
Including transcriptions
For arrangements of works for piano, 1 hand, see M26+
32.8 Collections
Operas, oratorios, cantatas, etc.
Class here piano scores
For piano music for radio, see M1527.5
For piano music for silent films and music not intended for specific motion picture sound tracks, see M176
For piano music for specific motion picture sound tracks, see M1527+
For piano music for television, see M1527.7+
For piano scores and piano-vocal scores of ballets, see M1523
For piano-vocal scores of operas, see M1503+
33 Complete works
33.5 Excerpts
34 Transcriptions, paraphrases (generally for concert purposes) of operas, oratorios, cantatas, excerpts, etc.
For potpourris, medleys, fantasies on operas, etc., see M39
Orchestral music. Band music
Class here arrangements of symphonies, suites, overtures, marches, dances, etc., and detached overtures, entr'actes, etc.
For arrangements of orchestral potpourris, etc., see M39
35 Complete works
35.5 Excerpts
Concertos, etc.
Class here concertos arranged for one piano (solo(s) and accompaniment)
For concertos in which the accompaniment is arranged for piano, the solo part(s) remaining unchanged, see the appropriate classes for solo(s) with piano
37 Complete works
37.5 Excerpts

	Instrumental music
	Solo instruments
	Piano
	Arrangements -- Continued
38	Chamber music, part-songs, and music for one instrument
38.2	Works for double keyboard, Janko keyboard, Solovox, etc.
38.3	Simplified editions of piano music for two hands
38.5	Songs
	Cf. M34, Transcriptions, paraphrases of operas, etc.
39	Potpourris. Medleys
	Including orchestra potpourris, etc., arranged for piano two hands
	For works with title "Theme and variations," "Variations on ...," etc., see M27
39.5	Works for two pianos, one performer
39.6	Works for piano, 1 hand
	Stringed instruments
40-44	Violin (Table M2)
44.3	Simplified editions
45-49	Viola (Table M2)
50-54	Violoncello (Table M2)
54.3	Simplified editions
	Double bass
55	Miscellaneous collections
	Original compositions
56	Collections
57	Separate works
58	Arrangements
	Class here collections and separate works
59.A-Z	Other, A-Z
59.B4	Baryton
59.C36	Campanula
59.C5	Ching hu
59.E7	Erh hu
59.H3	Haegŭm
59.H37	Hardanger fiddle
59.L9	Lyra viol
59.N3	Nan hu
59.P3	Pan hu
59.V53	Viol
59.V54	Viola da gamba
59.V56	Viola d'amore
59.5	Unspecified stringed instrument
	Wind instruments
60-64	Flute. Alto flute (Table M2)
65-69	Oboe (Table M2)
70-74	Clarinet. Bass (Alto, etc.) clarinet. Basset clarinet (Table M2)
75-79	Bassoon. Contrabassoon (Table M2)
80-84	Horn (Table M2)

	Instrumental music
	Solo instruments
	Wind instruments -- Continued
85-89	Trumpet. Cornet (Table M2)
90-94	Trombone. Bass trombone (Table M2)
95-99	Tuba (Table M2)
100-104	Saxhorn (Table M2)
105-109	Saxophone (Table M2)
110.A-Z	Other, A-Z
110.A47	Alphorn
	Bagpipe, see M145
110.B33	Baritone. Euphonium
110.B35	Basset horn
110.B57	Birbynė
110.C5	Coach horn
110.C78	Crumhorn
110.E5	English horn
	Euphonium, see M110.B33
110.F43	Fife
110.F5	Flageolet
110.F52	Flaviol
110.F53	Flügelhorn
110.H4	Heckelphone
110.H7	Hsiao
110.K4	Kaval
110.K8	Kuan
110.L9	Lur
110.M44	Melodica
110.O3	Ocarina
110.P36	Panpipes
110.P46	Penny whistle
110.P5	Piccolo
(110.P54)	P'illyul See M110.P58
110.P56	Pipe
110.P58	P'iri. P'illyul
110.R4	Recorder
110.S45	Shakuhachi
110.S47	Shehnai
110.S5	Shofar
110.S6	So na
110.T3	Taegŭm
110.T36	Tanso
110.T6	Ti tzu
111	Unspecified wind instrument
	Plucked instruments
115-119	Harp (Table M2)
120-124	Banjo (Table M2)
125-129	Guitar (Table M2)
130-134	Mandolin (Table M2)
135-139	Zither (Table M2)
	Lute
140	Collections

	Instrumental music
	Solo instruments
	Plucked instruments
	Lute -- Continued
141	Separate works
142.A-Z	Other, A-Z
142.A7	Appalachian dulcimer
142.A8	Archlute
142.B2	Balalaika
142.B3	Bandurria
142.B33	Bass guitar
142.B5	Biwa
142.C44	Celtic harp
142.C49	Cheng
142.C5	Ch'in
142.C58	Cittern
142.D55	Dobro
142.D6	Dömbra
	Dulcimer, see M175.D84
	Dulcimer, Appalachian, see M142.A7
142.E4	Electric guitar
142.E5	English guitar
142.G8	Gusli
142.H2	Harp-lute
142.H3	Hawaiian guitar
142.H9	Hyŏn' gŭm
142.I3	Ichigenkin
142.K36	Kanklės
142.K37	Kantele
142.K39	Kayagŭm
142.K55	Kobza
142.K58	Kŏmun'go
142.K59	Kopuz
142.K595	Kora
142.K6	Koto
142.M25	Mandola
142.M3	Mbira
142.O9	Oud
142.P6	P'i p'a
142.S45	Shamisen
142.S5	Sitar
142.T25	Tambura
142.T3	Tar (Lute)
142.U5	Ukulele
142.V53	Vihuela
142.V55	Vina
(142.Y35)	Yang ch'in See M175.Y3
142.Y83	Yüeh ch'in
	Percussion instruments. Other instruments
145	Bagpipe

Instrumental music
Solo instruments
Percussion instruments.
Other instruments -- Continued

146	Drum(s)
	Including timpani, drum set, side drum, etc., and works for two or more different percussion instruments
147	Bells, glockenspiel, etc.
	Children's instruments, see M1420
154	Concertina
165	Glass harmonica
172	Carillons. Chimes
174.A-Z	Mechanical instruments, A-Z
174.B37	Barrel organ
174.M85	Music box
175.A-Z	Other, A-Z
175.A4	Accordion
175.A5	Apollo harp
175.A8	Autoharp
175.B17	Bambuso sonoro
175.B2	Bandonion. Bayan
	Barrel organ, see M174.B37
	Bayan, see M175.B2
175.C3	Calliope
175.C35	Castanets
175.C44	Celesta
175.C5	Cimbalom
175.C54	Clavioline
	Concertina, see M154
175.D84	Dulcimer
175.H3	Harmonica
175.H9	Hurdy-gurdy
175.J4	Jew's harp
(175.L87)	Lur
	See M110.L9
175.M3	Mandolin harp
	Marimba, see M175.X6
175.M38	Melodeon
175.M9	Musical saw
175.O5	Ondes Martenot
175.O6	Orphéal
175.S26	Santūr
175.S5	Sheng
175.S55	Shō
175.T56	Tinglik
	Vibraharp, see M175.X6
	Vibraphone, see M175.X6
175.X6	Xylophone. Marimba. Vibraharp. Vibraphone
175.Y3	Yang ch'in
175.Y36	Yanggŭm
175.3	Whistling pieces

Instrumental music
Solo instruments
Percussion instruments.
Other instruments -- Continued
175.5 Unspecified solo instrument
For music for unspecified stringed instrument, see M59.5
For music for unspecified wind instrument, see M111
176 Instrumental music for motion pictures
Class here music for silent films and music not intended for specific motion pictures
For music composed for specific motion picture sound tracks, see M1527+
176.5 Instrumental music for radio and television
Class here music not intended for specific programs
For music composed for specific radio programs, see M1527.5+
For music composed for specific television programs, see M1527.7+
Music for two or more solo instruments
Class here chamber music and other ensemble music principally for one player to a part
For guidelines on classifying parts and scores with parts, see Score in the Glossary and General Guidelines following the Introduction
Cf. M990, chamber music for instruments of the 18th century and earlier that are generally not used in the modern symphony orchestra
Collections of two or more different combinations
177 Miscellaneous collections
178 Original compositions
179 Arrangements
Duets
Organ
Class here works for one or more organs, two or more players
180 Collections
181 Separate works
182-186 Organ and one other instrument (Table M2)
190 Reed organ
Class here works for two reed organs, or reed organ, four hands
191-195 Reed organ and one other instrument (Table M2)
198 Piano, three hands
Piano, four hands
200 Miscellaneous collections
Original compositions
201 General collections
Special collections. Separate works
202 Sonatas
203 Suites. Variations

Instrumental music
Music for two or more solo instruments
Duets
Piano, four hands
Original compositions
Special collections.
Separate works -- Continued
204 Pieces
Class here separate works only
Arrangements
207 Miscellaneous collections
Separate works
Operas, ballets, oratorios, cantatas, etc.
208 Complete works
208.5 Excerpts
209 Orchestral music. Band music
Including detached overtures
210 Concertos, etc.
211 Chamber music. Songs. Part-songs
212 Potpourris, etc. and single transcriptions or excerpts
Cf. M39, Potpourris, medleys, etc., for solo piano
For detached overtures, see M209
213 Piano, five or more hands
Two pianos, two performers
For two pianos, one performer, see M25.3
214 Original compositions
215 Arrangements
216 Two or more pianos, three or more performers
Piano and one other instrument
For guidelines on classifying works with continuo, see Continuo in the Glossary and General Guidelines following the Introduction
For piano and organ, see M182+
For piano and reed organ, see M191+
Piano and one stringed instrument
Piano and violin
217 Miscellaneous collections
Original compositions
218 General collections
Special collections. Separate works
219 Sonatas
220 Suites. Variations
221 Pieces
Class here separate works only
Arrangements
222 Collections
223 Separate works
224-228 Piano and viola (Table M2)
Piano and violoncello
229 Miscellaneous collections
Original compositions

Instrumental music
Music for two or more solo instruments
Duets
Piano and one other instrument
Piano and one stringed instrument
Piano and violoncello
Original compositions -- Continued
230 General collections
Special collections. Separate works
231 Sonatas
232 Suites. Variations
233 Pieces
Class here separate works only
Arrangements
235 Collections
236 Separate works
Piano and double bass
237 Collections
238 Separate works
239.A-Z Piano and one other stringed instrument. By stringed instrument, A-Z
239.P37 Pardessus de viole
(239.Q6) Quinton
See M239.P37
239.V54 Viola da gamba
239.V56 Viola d'amore
239.V58 Viola pomposa
239.V62 Violone
Piano and one wind instrument
240-244 Piano and flute. Piano and alto flute (Table M2)
Piano and oboe
245 Collections
Separate works
246 Original compositions
247 Arrangements
248-252 Piano and clarinet. Piano and bass (alto, etc.) clarinet. Piano and basset clarinet (Table M2)
Piano and bassoon. Piano and contrabassoon
253 Collections
254 Separate works
255-259 Piano and horn (Table M2)
Piano and trumpet. Piano and cornet
260 Collections
261 Separate works
Piano and trombone. Piano and bass trombone
262 Collections
263 Separate works
Piano and tuba
264 Collections
265 Separate works
Piano and saxhorn

Instrumental music
Music for two or more solo instruments
Duets
Piano and one other instrument
Piano and one wind instrument
Piano and saxhorn -- Continued
266 Collections
267 Separate works
Piano and saxophone
268 Collections
269 Separate works
Piano and one other wind instrument. By wind instrument, A-Z
270.A-Z Collections
270.A4 Alto horn
270.B3 Bagpipe
270.B37 Baritone. Euphonium
270.B4 Basset horn
270.B8 Bugle
270.C6 Cornett
270.E5 English horn
Euphonium, see M270.B37
270.F7 Flügelhorn
270.M4 Mellophone
270.O26 Oboe d'amore
270.O3 Ocarina
270.P3 Panpipes
270.P45 Piccolo
270.P5 Pipe
270.R4 Recorder
270.S45 Shakuhachi
270.S47 Shinobue
270.S5 Shofar
(270.S95) Syrinx
See M270.P3
270.T3 Tárogató
270.T45 Tenor horn
271.A-Z Separate works
271.A4 Alto horn
271.B3 Bagpipe
271.B37 Baritone. Euphonium
271.B4 Basset horn
271.B8 Bugle
271.C6 Cornett
271.E5 English horn
Euphonium, see M271.B37
271.F7 Flügelhorn
271.M4 Mellophone
271.O26 Oboe d'amore
271.O3 Ocarina
271.P3 Panpipes
271.P45 Piccolo
271.P5 Pipe

Instrumental music
  Music for two or more solo instruments
    Duets
      Piano and one other instrument
        Piano and one wind instrument
          Piano and one other wind instrument. By wind instrument, A-Z
            Separate works -- Continued
271.R4 Recorder
271.S45 Shakuhachi
271.S47 Shinobue
271.S5 Shofar
(271.S95) Syrinx
  See ML271.P3
271.T3 Tárogató
271.T45 Tenor horn
        Piano and one plucked instrument
          Piano and harp
272 Collections
273 Separate works
          Piano and banjo
274 Collections
275 Separate works
          Piano and guitar
276 Collections
277 Separate works
          Piano and mandolin
278 Collections
279 Separate works
          Piano and zither
280 Collections
281 Separate works
          Piano and one other plucked instrument. By plucked instrument, A-Z
282.A-Z Collections
282.B3 Balalaika
282.D64 Dömbra
  Dulcimer, see M284.D85
282.H4 Harp-lute guitar
282.L88 Lute
282.T3 Tar (Lute)
283.A-Z Separate works
283.B3 Balalaika
283.D64 Dömbra
  Dulcimer, see M285.D85
283.H4 Harp-lute guitar
283.L88 Lute
283.T3 Tar (Lute)
        Piano and other. By other instrument, A-Z
284.A-Z Collections
284.A3 Accordion
284.B33 Bandonion
284.B4 Bells

Instrumental music
Music for two or more solo instruments
Duets
Piano and one other instrument
Piano and other. By other instrument, A-Z
Collections -- Continued

284.C4 Celesta
284.C45 Cimbalom
284.C5 Clavioline
284.C6 Computer. Synthesizer
284.C94 Cymbals
284.D8 Drum
284.D85 Dulcimer
284.E4 Electronic instrument
Including pre-recorded tape
284.G6 Glass harmonica
284.G65 Glockenspiel
284.H3 Harmonica
Kettledrums, see M284.T5
Marimba, see M284.X9
284.O5 Ondes Martenot
284.P4 Percussion
Class here works for one percussionist playing two or more different percussion instruments
Piano accordion, see M284.A3
Synthesizer, see M284.C6
Tape, see M284.E4
284.T5 Timpani
Vibraphone, see M284.X9
284.X9 Xylophone. Marimba. Vibraphone
285.A-Z Separate works
285.A3 Accordion
285.B33 Bandonion
285.B4 Bells
285.C4 Celesta
285.C45 Cimbalom
285.C5 Clavioline
285.C6 Computer. Synthesizer
285.C94 Cymbals
285.D8 Drum
285.D85 Dulcimer
285.E4 Electronic instrument
Including pre-recorded tape
285.G6 Glass harmonica
285.G65 Glockenspiel
285.H3 Harmonica
Kettledrums, see M285.T5
Marimba, see M285.X9
285.O5 Ondes Martenot

Instrumental music
Music for two or more solo instruments
Duets
Piano and one other instrument
Piano and other. By other instrument, A-Z
Separate works -- Continued
285.P4 Percussion
Class here works for one percussionist playing two or more different percussion instruments
Piano accordion, see M285.A3
Synthesizer, see M285.C6
Tape, see M285.E4
285.T5 Timpani
Vibraphone, see M285.X9
285.X9 Xylophone. Marimba. Vibraphone
Piano and unspecified melody instrument
285.5 Collections
285.6 Separate works
Two stringed instruments
286 Collections
287 Separate works
Two wind instruments
288 Collections
289 Separate works
One stringed and one wind instrument
290 Collections
291 Separate works
Two plucked instruments
292 Collections
293 Separate works
One stringed and one plucked instrument
294 Collections
295 Separate works
One wind and one plucked instrument
296 Collections
297 Separate works
298 Other combinations of specified instruments
For accordion duets, see M1362
298.5 Unspecified instruments. Combinations of specified and unspecified instruments
Trios
For organ(s), three players, see M180+
300-304 Organ and two other instruments (Table M2)
305-309 Reed organ and two other instruments (Table M2)
Piano and two other instruments
For two or more pianos, three or more performers, see M216
Piano and two stringed instruments
310 Miscellaneous collections
Original compositions
311 General collections
Special collections. Separate works

Instrumental music
Music for two or more solo instruments
Trios
Piano and two other instruments
Piano and two stringed instruments
Original compositions
Special collections.
Separate works -- Continued
312 Piano, violin or viola, and violoncello
312.4 Other combinations
Class here separate works only
Arrangements
313 Collections
314 Separate works
315-319 Piano and two wind instruments (Table M2)
320-324 Piano, one stringed, and one wind instrument (Table M2)
325-329 Piano and two plucked instruments (Table M2)
330-334 Piano, one stringed, and one plucked instrument (Table M2)
335-339 Piano, one wind, and one plucked instrument (Table M2)
340-344 Piano and other combinations (Table M2)
349-353 Stringed instruments (Table M2)
Wind instruments
355 Miscellaneous collections
Original compositions
356 Collections
Separate works
357 General
357.2 Woodwinds only
357.4 Brasses only
Arrangements
358 Collections
359 Separate works
360-364 Stringed and wind instruments (Table M2)
365-369 Plucked instruments (Table M2)
370-374 Stringed and plucked instruments (Table M2)
375-379 Wind and plucked instruments (Table M2)
380-384 Stringed, wind, and plucked instruments (Table M2)
385 Other combinations of specified instruments
Including one or more performers playing two or more percussion instruments
386 Unspecified instruments. Combinations of specified and unspecified instruments
Quartets
400-404 Organ and three other instruments (Table M2)
405-409 Reed organ and three other instruments (Table M2)
Piano and three other instruments
Piano and three stringed instruments
410 Miscellaneous collections

Instrumental music
Music for two or more solo instruments
Quartets
Piano and three other instruments
Piano and three stringed instruments -- Continued
Original compositions
411 General collections
Special collections. Separate works
412 Piano, violin, viola, and violoncello
412.2 Piano and three violins
412.4 Piano and other combinations
Class here separate works only
Arrangements
413 Collections
414 Separate works
415-419 Piano and three wind instruments (Table M2)
420-424 Piano and three stringed and wind instruments (Table M2)
425-429 Piano and three plucked instruments (Table M2)
430-434 Piano and three stringed and plucked instruments (Table M2)
435-439 Piano and three wind and plucked instruments (Table M2)
440-444 Piano and three stringed, wind, and plucked instruments (Table M2)
445-449 Piano and other combinations (Table M2)
Stringed instruments
450 Miscellaneous collections
Original compositions
451 General collections
Special collections. Separate works
452 Two violins, viola, and violoncello
452.2 Four violins
452.4 Other combinations
Class here separate works only
Arrangements
453 Collections
454 Separate works
Wind instruments
455 Miscellaneous collections
Original compositions
456 Collections
Separate works
457 General
457.2 Woodwinds only
457.4 Brasses only
Arrangements
458 Collections
459 Separate works
460-464 Stringed and wind instruments (Table M2)
465-469 Plucked instruments (Table M2)

Instrumental music
Music for two or more solo instruments
Quartets -- Continued
470-474 Stringed and plucked instruments (Table M2)
475-479 Wind and plucked instruments (Table M2)
480-484 Stringed, wind, and plucked instruments (Table M2)
485 Other combinations of specified instruments
Including one or more performers playing two or more percussion instruments
486 Unspecified instruments. Combinations of specified and unspecified instruments
Quintets
500-504 Organ and four other instruments (Table M2)
505-509 Reed organ and four other instruments (Table M2)
Piano and four other instruments
Piano and four stringed instruments
510 Miscellaneous collections
Original compositions
511 General collections
Special collections. Separate works
512 Piano, two violins, viola, and violoncello
512.2 Piano and four violins
512.4 Piano and other combinations
Class here separate works only
Arrangements
513 Collections
514 Separate works
515-519 Piano and four wind instruments (Table M2)
520-524 Piano and four stringed and wind instruments (Table M2)
525-529 Piano and four plucked instruments (Table M2)
530-534 Piano and four stringed and plucked instruments (Table M2)
535-539 Piano and four wind and plucked instruments (Table M2)
540-544 Piano and four stringed, wind, and plucked instruments (Table M2)
545-549 Piano and other combinations (Table M2)
550-554 Stringed instruments (Table M2)
Wind instruments
555 Miscellaneous collections
Original compositions
556 Collections
Separate works
557 General
557.2 Woodwinds only
557.4 Brasses only
Arrangements
558 Collections
559 Separate works
560-564 Stringed and wind instruments (Table M2)

Instrumental music
Music for two or more solo instruments
Quintets -- Continued
565-569 Plucked instruments (Table M2)
570-574 Stringed and plucked instruments (Table M2)
575-579 Wind and plucked instruments (Table M2)
580-584 Stringed, wind, and plucked instruments (Table M2)
585 Other combinations of specified instruments
Including one or more performers playing two or more percussion instruments
586 Unspecified instruments. Combinations of specified and unspecified instruments
Sextets
600-604 Organ and five other instruments (Table M2)
605-609 Reed organ and five other instruments (Table M2)
Piano and five other instruments
610-614 Piano and five stringed instruments (Table M2)
615-619 Piano and five wind instruments (Table M2)
620-624 Piano and five stringed and wind instruments (Table M2)
625-629 Piano and five plucked instruments (Table M2)
630-634 Piano and five stringed and plucked instruments (Table M2)
635-639 Piano and five wind and plucked instruments (Table M2)
640-644 Piano and five stringed, wind, and plucked instruments (Table M2)
645-649 Piano and other combinations (Table M2)
650-654 Stringed instruments (Table M2)
Wind instruments
655 Miscellaneous collections
Original compositions
656 Collections
Separate works
657 General
657.2 Woodwinds only
657.4 Brasses only
Arrangements
658 Collections
659 Separate works
660-664 Stringed and wind instruments (Table M2)
665-669 Plucked instruments (Table M2)
670-674 Stringed and plucked instruments (Table M2)
675-679 Wind and plucked instruments (Table M2)
680-684 Stringed, wind, and plucked instruments (Table M2)
685 Other combinations of specified instruments
Including one or more performers playing two or more percussion instruments

Instrumental music
Music for two or more solo instruments
Sextets -- Continued
686 Unspecified instruments. Combinations of specified and unspecified instruments
Septets
700-704 Organ and six other instruments (Table M2)
705-709 Reed organ and six other instruments (Table M2)
Piano and six other instruments
710-714 Piano and six stringed instruments (Table M2)
715-719 Piano and six wind instruments (Table M2)
720-724 Piano and six stringed and wind instruments (Table M2)
725-729 Piano and six plucked instruments (Table M2)
730-734 Piano and six stringed and plucked instruments (Table M2)
735-739 Piano and six wind and plucked instruments (Table M2)
740-744 Piano and six stringed, wind, and plucked instruments (Table M2)
745-749 Piano and other combinations (Table M2)
750-754 Stringed instruments (Table M2)
Wind instruments
755 Miscellaneous collections
Original compositions
756 Collections
Separate works
757 General
757.2 Woodwinds only
757.4 Brasses only
Arrangements
758 Collections
759 Separate works
760-764 Stringed and wind instruments (Table M2)
765-769 Plucked instruments (Table M2)
770-774 Stringed and plucked instruments (Table M2)
775-779 Wind and plucked instruments (Table M2)
780-784 Stringed, wind, and plucked instruments (Table M2)
785 Other combinations of specified instruments
Including one or more performers playing two or more percussion instruments
786 Unspecified instruments. Combinations of specified and unspecified instruments
Octets
800-804 Organ and seven other instruments (Table M2)
805-809 Reed organ and seven other instruments (Table M2)
Piano and seven other instruments
810-814 Piano and seven stringed instruments (Table M2)
815-819 Piano and seven wind instruments (Table M2)

Instrumental music
Music for two or more solo instruments
Octets
Piano and seven other instruments -- Continued
820-824 Piano and seven stringed and wind instruments (Table M2)
825-829 Piano and seven plucked instruments (Table M2)
830-834 Piano and seven stringed and plucked instruments (Table M2)
835-839 Piano and seven wind and plucked instruments (Table M2)
840-844 Piano and seven stringed, wind, and plucked instruments (Table M2)
845-849 Piano and other combinations (Table M2)
850-854 Stringed instruments (Table M2)
Wind instruments
855 Miscellaneous collections
Original compositions
856 Collections
Separate works
857 General
857.2 Woodwinds only
857.4 Brasses only
Arrangements
858 Collections
859 Separate works
860-864 Stringed and wind instruments (Table M2)
865-869 Plucked instruments (Table M2)
870-874 Stringed and plucked instruments (Table M2)
875-879 Wind and plucked instruments (Table M2)
880-884 Stringed, wind, and plucked instruments (Table M2)
885 Other combinations of specified instruments
Including one or more performers playing two or more percussion instruments
886 Unspecified instruments. Combinations of specified and unspecified instruments
Nonets and larger chamber music combinations
900-904 Organ and eight or more other instruments (Table M2)
905-909 Reed organ and eight or more other instruments
Piano and eight or more other instruments
910-914 Piano and eight or more stringed instruments (Table M2)
915-919 Piano and eight or more wind instruments (Table M2)
920-924 Piano and eight or more stringed and wind instruments (Table M2)
925-929 Piano and eight or more plucked instruments (Table M2)
930-934 Piano and eight or more stringed and plucked instruments (Table M2)

Instrumental music
Music for two or more solo instruments
Nonets and larger chamber music combinations
Piano and eight or more other instruments -- Continued
935-939 Piano and eight or more wind and plucked instruments (Table M2)
940-944 Piano and eight or more stringed, wind, and plucked instruments (Table M2)
945-949 Piano and other combinations (Table M2)
950-954 Stringed instruments (Table M2)
Wind instruments
955 Miscellaneous collections
Original compositions
956 Collections
Separate works
957 General
957.2 Woodwinds only
957.4 Brasses only
Arrangements
958 Collections
959 Separate works
960-964 Stringed and wind instruments (Table M2)
965-969 Plucked instruments (Table M2)
970-974 Stringed and plucked instruments (Table M2)
975-979 Wind and plucked instruments (Table M2)
980-984 Stringed, wind, and plucked instruments (Table M2)
985 Other combinations of specified instruments
Including one or more performers playing two or more percussion instruments
986 Unspecified instruments. Combinations of specified and unspecified instruments
990 Chamber music for instruments of the 18th century and earlier that are generally not used in the modern symphony orchestra, including viol, viola d'amore, crumhorn, recorder, etc.
Class here works for two or more such instruments, specified or unspecified, with or without organ or piano (continuo)
For one instrument and organ (continuo), see M182+
For chamber music of the Baroque and later periods for recorders, see M355-M359, M455-M459, etc.
For ensembles of early instruments with other instruments, see M177-M986
For one instrument and piano (continuo), see M239, M270-M271, M282-M283, M284-M285
Orchestra
Including works for chamber orchestra
1000 Miscellaneous collections. General collections
Original compositions
Including special collections

Instrumental music
Orchestra
Original compositions -- Continued
1001 Symphonies
1002 Symphonic poems
1003 Suites. Variations
Including separately published suites from operas, ballets, etc.
1004 Overtures
Including separately published opera preludes, entr'actes, and overtures
Solo instrument(s) with orchestra
Including concertos, etc.
Class here original works and arrangements
1004.5 Collections for different solo instruments
Class here scores and solo(s) with piano
Collections of cadenzas
1004.6 Different solo instruments
1004.7.A-Z Specific solo instruments. By instrument, A-Z
Single solo instruments and two or more like solo instruments
Organ
1005 Scores
Class here full and reduced scores
Including arrangements for reduced orchestra
1005.5.A-Z Cadenzas
By composer of concerto, A-Z
1006 Solo(s) with piano
Piano
1010 Scores
Class here full and reduced scores
Including arrangements for reduced orchestra
1010.5.A-Z Cadenzas. By composer of concerto, A-Z
1011 Solo(s) with piano
Stringed instruments
Violin
1012 Scores
Class here full and reduced scores
Including arrangements for reduced orchestra
1012.5.A-Z Cadenzas. By composer of concerto, A-Z
1013 Solo(s) with piano
Viola
1014 Scores
Class here full and reduced scores
Including arrangements for reduced orchestra
1014.5.A-Z Cadenzas. By composer of concerto, A-Z
1015 Solo(s) with piano
Violoncello

Instrumental music
Orchestra
Original compositions
Solo instrument(s) with orchestra
Single solo instruments
and two or more like solo instruments
Stringed instruments
Violoncello -- Continued

1016 Scores
Class here full and reduced scores
Including arrangements for reduced orchestra

1016.5.A-Z Cadenzas. By composer of concerto, A-Z

1017 Solo(s) with piano

1018 Double bass
Class here scores, cadenzas, and solo(s) with piano

1019.A-Z Other, A-Z
Class here scores, cadenzas, and solo(s) with piano

1019.C5 Ching hu

1019.C55 Chung hu

1019.E8 Erh hu

1019.K32 Kao hu

1019.P3 Pan hu

1019.V54 Viola da gamba

1019.V56 Viola d'amore

Wind instruments
Flute. Alto flute

1020 Scores
Class here full and reduced scores
Including arrangements for reduced orchestra

1020.5.A-Z Cadenzas. By composer of concerto, A-Z

1021 Solo(s) with piano

Oboe

1022 Scores
Class here full and reduced scores
Including arrangements for reduced orchestra

1022.5.A-Z Cadenzas. By composer of concerto, A-Z

1023 Solo(s) with piano

Clarinet. Bass (Alto, etc.) clarinet. Basset clarinet

1024 Scores
Class here full and reduced scores
Including arrangements for reduced orchestra

1024.5.A-Z Cadenzas. By composer of concerto, A-Z

1025 Solo(s) with piano

Bassoon. Contrabassoon

Instrumental music
Orchestra
Original compositions
Solo instrument(s) with orchestra
Single solo instruments
and two or more like solo instruments
Wind instruments
Bassoon. Contrabassoon -- Continued
1026 Scores
Class here full and reduced scores
Including arrangements for reduced orchestra
1026.5.A-Z Cadenzas. By composer of concerto, A-Z
1027 Solo(s) with piano
Horn
1028 Scores
Class here full and reduced scores
Including arrangements for reduced orchestra
1028.5.A-Z Cadenzas. By composer of concerto, A-Z
1029 Solo(s) with piano
Trumpet. Cornet
1030 Scores
Class here full and reduced scores
Including arrangements for reduced orchestra
1030.5.A-Z Cadenzas. By composer of concerto, A-Z
1031 Solo(s) with piano
Trombone. Bass trombone
1032 Scores
Class here full and reduced scores
Including arrangements for reduced orchestra
1032.5.A-Z Cadenzas. By composer of concerto, A-Z
1033 Solo(s) with piano
Other, A-Z
1034.A-Z Scores
Class here full and reduced scores
Including arrangements for reduced orchestra
1034.B37 Baritone. Euphonium
1034.B38 Basset horn
1034.C5 Chalumeau
1034.E5 English horn
Euphonium, see M1034.B37
1034.F6 Flügelhorn
1034.H4 Heckelphone
1034.K8 Kuan
1034.O26 Oboe d'amore
1034.P5 Piccolo
1034.R4 Recorder
1034.R66 Roopill
1034.S4 Saxophone

Instrumental music
Orchestra
Original compositions
Solo instrument(s) with orchestra
Single solo instruments
and two or more like solo instruments
Wind instruments
Other, A-Z
Scores -- Continued

1034.S5 Shakuhachi
1034.T3 Tárogató
1034.T6 Ti tzu
1034.T8 Tuba
1034.5.A-Z Cadenzas. By composer of cadenza, A-Z
1034.5.B37 Baritone. Euphonium
1034.5.B38 Basset horn
1034.5.C5 Chalumeau
1034.5.E5 English horn
Euphonium, see M1034.5.B37
1034.5.F6 Flügelhorn
1034.5.H4 Heckelphone
1034.5.K8 Kuan
1034.5.O26 Oboe d'amore
1034.5.P5 Piccolo
1034.5.R4 Recorder
1034.5.R66 Roopill
1034.5.S4 Saxophone
1034.5.S5 Shakuhachi
1034.5.T3 Tárogató
1034.5.T6 Ti tzu
1034.5.T8 Tuba
1035.A-Z Solo(s) with piano
1035.B37 Baritone. Euphonium
1035.B38 Basset horn
1035.C5 Chalumeau
1035.E5 English horn
Euphonium, see M1035.B37
1035.F6 Flügelhorn
1035.H4 Heckelphone
1035.K8 Kuan
1035.O26 Oboe d'amore
1035.P5 Piccolo
1035.R4 Recorder
1035.R66 Roopill
1035.S4 Saxophone
1035.S5 Shakuhachi
1035.T3 Tárogató
1035.T6 Ti tzu
1035.T8 Tuba

Plucked instruments
Harp

Instrumental music
Orchestra
Original compositions
Solo instrument(s) with orchestra
Single solo instruments
and two or more like solo instruments
Plucked instruments
Harp -- Continued
1036 Scores
Class here full and reduced scores
Including arrangements for reduced orchestra
1036.5.A-Z Cadenzas. By composer of concerto, A-Z
1037 Solo(s) with piano
1037.4.A-Z Other, A-Z
Class here scores, cadenzas, and solo(s) with piano
1037.4.B3 Balalaika
1037.4.C3 Canun
1037.4.C58 Cithara
1037.4.D64 Dömbra
1037.4.G8 Guitar
1037.4.K68 Koto
1037.4.M3 Mandolin
1037.4.P5 P‘i p‘a
1037.4.S58 Sitar
1037.4.T3 Tar (Lute)
1037.4.U4 Ukulele
1037.4.Z6 Zither
Percussion instruments
1038 Scores
Class here full and reduced scores
Including arrangements for reduced orchestra
1038.5.A-Z Cadenzas. By composer of concerto, A-Z
1039 Solo(s) with piano
1039.4.A-Z Other instruments, A-Z
Class here scores, cadenzas, and solo(s) with piano
1039.4.A3 Accordion
1039.4.B3 Bandonion
1039.4.B4 Bayan
1039.4.C55 Cimbalom
1039.4.D85 Dulcimer
1039.4.E35 Electronic instrument
Class here works for one performer using two or more different electronic instruments or devices, or for electronic media that cannot be assigned a more specific class, e.g., M1039.4.O5, Ondes Martenot; M1039.4.S95, Synthesizer
1039.4.E37 Electronic organ

Instrumental music
Orchestra
Original compositions
Solo instrument(s) with orchestra
Single solo instruments
and two or more like solo instruments
Other instruments, A-Z -- Continued

(1039.4.E38) Electronics
See M1039.4.E35, Electronic instrument

1039.4.E4 Electronium
1039.4.H3 Harmonica
1039.4.H87 Hurdy-gurdy
1039.4.O5 Ondes Martenot
1039.4.P5 Pianola
Pre-recorded tape, see M1039.4.T3
1039.4.S5 Sheng
1039.4.S95 Synthesizer
1039.4.T3 Tape
Including pre-recorded tape
1039.4.T7 Trautonium
1039.4.X9 Xylophone
1039.4.Y35 Yang ch'in
1039.5 Unspecified instrument
Class here scores, cadenzas, and solos with piano

Two or more different solo instruments
1040 Scores
Class here full and reduced scores
Including arrangements for reduced orchestra
1040.5.A-Z Cadenzas. By composer of concerto, A-Z
1041 Solos with piano
1042 Concertos for orchestra
Pieces
1045 General
1046 Marches
Dances
1047 General
1048 Two-rhythm (polka, etc.)
1049 Three-rhythm (waltz, etc.)

Arrangements
For arrangements for solo instrument(s) with orchestra, see M1004.5+

1060 General
1070 Excerpts
Including purely orchestral arrangements of operatic scenes for concert purposes
1075 Potpourris, fantaisies, etc.

String orchestra
1100 Miscellaneous collections. General collections
Original compositions
Including special collections
1101 Symphonies
1102 Symphonic poems

Instrumental music
String orchestra
Original compositions -- Continued
1103 Suites. Variations
1104 Overtures
Including separately published opera preludes, entr'actes, and overtures
Solo instrument(s) with string orchestra
Including concertos, etc.
Class here original works and arrangements
Collections for different solo instruments
1105 Scores
1106 Solo(s) with piano
Single solo instruments and two or more like solo instruments
Organ
1108 Scores
Class here full and reduced scores
Including arrangements for reduced string orchestra
1108.5.A-Z Cadenzas
By composer of concerto, A-Z
1109 Solo(s) with piano
Piano
1110 Scores
Class here full and reduced scores
Including arrangements for reduced string orchestra
1110.5.A-Z Cadenzas. By composer of concerto, A-Z
1111 Solo(s) with piano
Stringed instruments
Violin
1112 Scores
Class here full and reduced scores
Including arrangements for reduced string orchestra
1112.5.A-Z Cadenzas. By composer of concerto, A-Z
1113 Solo(s) with piano
Viola
1114 Scores
Class here full and reduced scores
Including arrangements for reduced string orchestra
1114.5.A-Z Cadenzas. By composer of concerto, A-Z
1115 Solo(s) with piano
Violoncello
1116 Scores
Class here full and reduced scores
Including arrangements for reduced string orchestra
1116.5.A-Z Cadenzas. By composer of concerto, A-Z
1117 Solo(s) with piano

Instrumental music
String orchestra
Original compositions
Solo instrument(s) with string orchestra
Single solo instruments
and two or more like solo instruments
Stringed instruments -- Continued

1118 Double bass
Class here scores, cadenzas, and solo(s) with piano

1119.A-Z Other, A-Z
Class here scores, cadenzas, and solo(s) with piano

1119.H37 Hardanger fiddle

1119.N36 Nan hu

1119.V54 Viola da gamba

1119.V56 Viola d'amore

1119.V6 Violoncello piccolo

Wind instruments
Flute. Alto flute

1120 Scores
Class here full and reduced scores
Including arrangements for reduced string orchestra

1120.5.A-Z Cadenzas. By composer of concerto, A-Z

1121 Solo(s) with piano

Oboe

1122 Scores
Class here full and reduced scores
Including arrangements for reduced string orchestra

1122.5.A-Z Cadenzas. By composer of concerto, A-Z

1123 Solo(s) with piano

Clarinet. Bass (Alto, etc.) clarinet. Basset clarinet

1124 Scores
Class here full and reduced scores
Including arrangements for reduced string orchestra

1124.5.A-Z Cadenzas. By composer of concerto, A-Z

1125 Solo(s) with piano

Bassoon. Contrabassoon

1126 Scores
Class here full and reduced scores
Including arrangements for reduced string orchestra

1126.5.A-Z Cadenzas. By composer of concerto, A-Z

1127 Solo(s) with piano

Horn

1128 Scores
Class here full and reduced scores
Including arrangements for reduced string orchestra

Instrumental music
String orchestra
Original compositions
Solo instrument(s) with string orchestra
Single solo instruments
and two or more like solo instruments
Wind instruments
Horn -- Continued
1128.5.A-Z Cadenzas. By composer of concerto, A-Z
1129 Solo(s) with piano
Trumpet. Cornet
1130 Scores
Class here full and reduced scores
Including arrangements for reduced string orchestra
1130.5.A-Z Cadenzas. By composer of concerto, A-Z
1131 Solo(s) with piano
Trombone. Bass trombone
1132 Scores
Class here full and reduced scores
Including arrangements for reduced string orchestra
1132.5.A-Z Cadenzas. By composer of concerto, A-Z
1133 Solo(s) with piano
Other, A-Z
1134.A-Z Scores
Class here full and reduced scores
Including arrangements for reduced string orchestra
1134.B37 Baritone. Euphonium
1134.E5 English horn
Euphonium, see M1134.B37
1134.F7 Flügelhorn
1134.O26 Oboe d'amore
1134.P5 Piccolo
1134.R4 Recorder
1134.S4 Saxophone
1134.S5 Shakuhachi
1134.T8 Tuba
Cadenzas. By composer of cadenza, A-Z
1134.5.B37 Baritone. Euphonium
1134.5.E5 English horn
Euphonium, see M1134.5.B37
1134.5.F7 Flügelhorn
1134.5.O26 Oboe d'amore
1134.5.P5 Piccolo
1134.5.R4 Recorder
1134.5.S4 Saxophone
1134.5.S5 Shakuhachi
1134.5.T8 Tuba
Solo(s) with piano
1135.B37 Baritone. Euphonium
1135.E5 English horn

Instrumental music
String orchestra
Original compositions
Solo instrument(s) with string orchestra
Single solo instruments
and two or more like solo instruments
Wind instruments
Other, A-Z
Solo(s) with piano -- Continued
Euphonium, see M1135.B37
1135.F7 Flügelhorn
1135.O26 Oboe d'amore
1135.P5 Piccolo
1135.R4 Recorder
1135.S4 Saxophone
1135.S5 Shakuhachi
1135.T8 Tuba
Plucked instruments
Harp
1136 Scores
Class here full and reduced scores
Including arrangements for reduced string orchestra
1136.5.A-Z Cadenzas. By composer of concerto, A-Z
1137 Solo(s) with piano
1137.4.A-Z Other, A-Z
Class here scores, cadenzas, and solo(s) with piano
1137.4.G8 Guitar
1137.4.L88 Lute
1137.4.M3 Mandolin
1137.4.O9 Oud
Percussion instruments
1138 Scores
Class here full and reduced scores
Including arrangements for reduced string orchestra
1138.5.A-Z Cadenzas. By composer of concerto, A-Z
1139 Solo(s) with piano
1139.4.A-Z Other instruments, A-Z
Class here scores, cadenzas, and solo(s) with piano
1139.4.A3 Accordion
1139.4.B3 Bandonion
1139.4.C6 Concertina
1139.4.H3 Harmonica
1139.4.O5 Ondes Martenot
1139.4.W5 Wind controller
1139.5 Unspecified solo instrument
Class here scores, cadenzas and solos with piano
Two or more different solo instruments

Instrumental music
String orchestra
Original compositions
Solo instrument(s) with string orchestra
Two or more different
solo instruments -- Continued
1140 Scores
Class here full and reduced scores
Including arrangements for reduced string orchestra
1140.5.A-Z Cadenzas. By composer of concerto, A-Z
1141 Solos with piano
1142 Concertos for string orchestra
Pieces
1145 General
1146 Marches
Dances
1147 General
1148 Two-rhythm (polka, etc.)
1149 Three-rhythm (waltz, etc.)
1160 Arrangements
For arrangements for solo instrument(s) with string orchestra, see M1105+
Band
1200 Miscellaneous collections. General collections
Original compositions
Including special collections
1201 Symphonies
1202 Symphonic poems
1203 Suites. Variations
1204 Overtures
Including separately published opera preludes, entr'actes, and overtures
Solo instrument(s) with band
1205 Scores
1206 Solo(s) with piano
1242 Concertos for band
Pieces
1245 General
1247 Marches
Dances
1247.9 General
1248 Two-rhythm (polka, etc.)
1249 Three-rhythm (waltzes, etc.)
Arrangements
1254 Symphonies, symphonic poems, suites, etc.
1255 Overtures
Including separately published opera preludes, entr'actes, and overtures
1257 Solo instrument(s) with band
Class here scores and solo(s) with piano
Pieces
1258 General

Instrumental music
Band
Arrangements
Pieces -- Continued
1260 Marches
Dances
1262 General
1264 Two-rhythm (polka, etc.)
1266 Three-rhythm (waltz, etc.)
1268 Potpourris, fantaisies, etc.
1269 Marching routines
1270 Fife (bugle) and drum music, field music, etc.
Reduced orchestra
Class here works for music hall, salon, etc., orchestra, in which the piano is generally the leading instrument
Including dance orchestra music received prior to July 1, 1944
For dance orchestra music received after July 1, 1944, see M1356+
For lead sheets, see M1356.2
1350 General
1353 Solos with accompaniment
Class here original compositions only
Dance orchestra and instrumental ensembles
Including popular music of all countries
For music copyrighted or received prior to July 1, 1944, see M1350+
1356 General
1356.2 Lead sheets
1360 Mandolin and similar orchestras of plucked instruments
1362 Accordion band
Including music for two or more accordions
1363 Steel band
1365 Minstrel music
Class here instrumental and vocal music
1366 Jazz ensembles
Class here instrumental duets, trios, etc.
For jazz for solo instruments, see M6+
Instrumental music for children
Solo instruments
1375 Organ. Reed organ
Piano
1378 Collections
1380 Separate works
1385.A-Z Other, A-Z
1385.A4 Accordion
1385.A8 Autoharp
1385.B34 Bandonion
1385.B35 Banjo
1385.C6 Clarinet
1385.D6 Double bass
1385.D7 Drum

Instrumental music
Instrumental music for children
Solo instruments
Other, A-Z -- Continued
1385.E4 Electronic organ
1385.F6 Flute
1385.G7 Guitar
1385.H3 Harp
1385.H6 Horn
Marimba, see M1385.X9
1385.M3 Melody instrument. Unspecified solo instrument
1385.P5 Percussion
Class here works for one percussionist playing two or more different percussion instruments
1385.R3 Recorder
1385.T76 Trombone
1385.T78 Trumpet
1385.T8 Tuba
1385.U5 Ukulele
Unspecified solo instrument, see M1385.M3
Vibraharp, see M1385.X9
Vibraphone, see M1385.X9
1385.V35 Viola
1385.V4 Violin
1385.V45 Violoncello
1385.X9 Xylophone. Marimba. Vibraharp. Vibraphone
Duets
Piano
Class here works for one or more pianos, two or more performers
1389 Collections
1390 Separate works
Piano and violin. Piano and viola
1393 Collections
1395 Separate works
1400 Piano and violoncello. Piano and double bass
1405 Piano and wind instrument
1410 Other
1413-1417 Trios, quartets, etc. (Table M2)
1420 Orchestral music. Band music
Including toy orchestra

Instrumental music -- Continued

1450 Dance music

Class here dances for unspecified medium of performance

Cf. GV1580+, Dancing (including dance instruction)

Cf. M1520+, Ballets, pantomimes, masques, pageants, etc.

Cf. M1627+, Folk, national, and ethnic dances

For music to accompany instruction in ballet, gymnastics, rhythmic movement, etc., see MT950

For dances for specific instrumental or vocal mediums of performance, see the appropriate class, e.g., Piano, M30-M32

1470 Chance compositions

Including works using any means of sound production

For chamber music for unspecified instruments, see M298.5, M386, M486, etc.

For works with a specified medium of performance, see the appropriate class, e.g., Piano, M20-M39

1473 Electronic music

Class here music intended for performance solely by means of electronic media, e.g., synthesizer, pre-recorded tape, etc.

For electronic organ, see M14.8+

For ondes Martenot, see M175.O5

For works for electric violin, see M40-M44.3; electric guitar, M125-M129, etc.

For works for instrument(s) and/or voice(s) with electronic sounds, see the class for the other instrument(s) or voice(s), e.g., electronic instrument and piano, M284.E4, M285.E4; quartets including electronic instrument(s) M485; songs with electronic instrument(s) M1613.3

1480 Music with color or light apparatus

1490 Music printed before 1700 or copied in manuscript before 1700

Class here instrumental and vocal music

For music printed or copied before 1700 in the American colonies, later the United States, see M1.A1+

Vocal music

1495 Collections

Class here miscellaneous collections of sacred and secular vocal music by two or more composers

For miscellaneous collections of sacred and secular vocal music by one composer, see M3.1

Secular vocal music

Vocal music
Secular vocal music -- Continued
1497 Collections
Class here miscellaneous collections of secular vocal music by two or more composers
For miscellaneous collections of secular vocal music by one composer, see M3.1
Dramatic music
Operas
Including operettas, Singspiele, sacred operas, musicals, etc.
For Chinese operas, see M1805.3+
For North Korean revolutionary operas, see M1819.3
Scores
1500 Complete works
1501 Concert arrangements
Vocal scores. Chorus scores
1502 Without accompaniment
Piano accompaniment
1503 General
1503.5 Concert arrangements
1504 College operas
Excerpts
Including vocal or predominantly vocal excerpts from works composed for specific motion picture sound tracks
Cf. M1527.2, Motion picture music excerpts
1505 Original accompaniment
Arranged accompaniment
1506 Orchestra or other ensemble
Piano
1507 Collections
1508 Separate works. By title
Vocal and chorus scores without accompaniment
1508.1 Collections
1508.2 Separate works
1509 Operatic scenes
Class here independent works
For opera excerpts, see M1505+
Incidental music
1510 Full scores
1512 Vocal and chorus scores without accompaniment
1513 Vocal scores with piano accompaniment
Excerpts
1515 Original accompaniment
Arranged accompaniment
1516 Orchestra or other ensemble
Piano
1517 Collections
1518 Separate works. By title

Vocal music
Secular vocal music
Dramatic music -- Continued
Ballets
Including pantomimes, masques, pageants, etc.
1520 Full scores
1522 Vocal and chorus scores without accompaniment
1523 Piano scores. Vocal scores with piano accompaniment
Excerpts
1524 Original accompaniment
Arranged accompaniment
1525 Orchestra or other ensemble
1526 Piano
Motion picture music
Class here music composed for specific motion picture sound tracks, including musicals either originally composed for motion pictures or adapted from stage versions
For music for silent films and music not intended for specific motion picture sound tracks, see M176
1527 Complete works
1527.2 Excerpts
Class here instrumental, or predominantly instrumental, excerpts
For vocal excerpts, see M1505+
Radio music
Class here music composed for specific programs
For music not intended for specific programs, see M176.5
1527.5 Complete works
Including vocal themes for programs
1527.6 Excerpts
Television music
Class here music composed for specific programs
For music not intended for specific programs, see M176.5
1527.7 Complete works
1527.8 Excerpts
Duets, trios, etc., for solo voices
Accompaniment of orchestra or other ensemble, or electric accompaniment
1528 Full scores
1528.5 Vocal scores without accompaniment
1529 Vocal scores with piano
Accompaniment of keyboard or other instrument, or unaccompanied
Class here works whose performance by solo voices is specifically indicated
For part-songs, glees, madrigals, etc., that may be performed by either solo voices or chorus, see M1547+

Vocal music
Secular vocal music
Duets, trios, etc., for solo voices
Accompaniment of keyboard
or other instrument,
or unaccompanied -- Continued
Duets
1529.2 Collections
1529.3 Separate works
Trios, quartets, etc.
1529.4 Collections
1529.5 Separate works
Choruses
Choruses with orchestra or other ensemble
Class here choruses with or without solo voices
Mixed voices
Full scores
Orchestral accompaniment
1530 General
1530.3 With recitation
1531 Other accompaniment
Class here works with accompaniment of string orchestra, band, other ensemble of two or more instruments, or electronic accompaniment
1532 Vocal and chorus scores without accompaniment
Vocal scores with piano accompaniment
1533 General
1533.3 With recitation
Excerpts
1534 Original accompaniment
Arranged accompaniment
1535 Orchestra or other ensemble
Piano
1536 Collections
1537 Separate works
Men's voices
Full scores
Orchestral accompaniment
1538 General
1538.3 With recitation
1539 Other accompaniment
Class here works with accompaniment of string orchestra, band, other ensemble of two or more instruments, or electronic accompaniment
Vocal scores with piano accompaniment
1540 General
1540.3 With recitation
Excerpts
1541 Orchestral accompaniment
1542 Piano accompaniment
Treble voices

Vocal music
Secular vocal music
Choruses
Choruses with orchestra or other ensemble
Treble voices -- Continued
Full scores
Orchestral accompaniment
1543 General
1543.3 With recitation
1543.5 Other accompaniment
Class here works with accompaniment of string orchestra, band, other ensemble of two or more instruments, or electronic accompaniment
Vocal scores with piano accompaniment
1544 General
1544.3 With recitation
Excerpts
1545 Accompaniment of orchestra or other ensemble
1546 Piano accompaniment
1546.5 Children's voices
Cf. M1997+, choruses, songs, etc., for children
Choruses, part-songs, etc., with accompaniment of keyboard or other solo instrument, or unaccompanied
Class here choruses, with or without solo voices, and part-songs, glees, madrigals, etc., that may be performed by either chorus or solo voices
For works whose performance by solo voices is specifically indicated, see M1529.2+
1547 Collections of accompanied and unaccompanied works
Accompaniment of keyboard instrument
Collections
Including collections that contain some works with accompaniment of other solo instrument
1548 Two or more types of chorus
1549 Mixed voices
1550 Men's voices
1551 Treble voices
Separate works
1552 Mixed voices
1560 Men's voices
1570 Treble voices
Accompaniment of instrument other than keyboard instrument
1574 Two or more types of chorus
Class here collections only
1575 Mixed voices
1576 Men's voices

Vocal music
Secular vocal music
Choruses
Choruses, part-songs, etc., with accompaniment of keyboard or other solo instrument, or unaccompanied
Accompaniment of instrument other than keyboard instrument -- Continued
1577 Treble voices
Unaccompanied works
Collections
1578 Two or more types of chorus
1579 Mixed voices
1580 Men's voices
1581 Treble voices
Separate works
1582 Mixed voices
1590 Men's voices
1600 Treble voices
1608 Choruses, etc., in tonic sol-fa notation
1609 Unison choruses
(1610) Cantatas, choral symphonies, etc., for unaccompanied chorus with or without solo voices
For unaccompanied sacred works, see M2081+
For unaccompanied secular works, see M1578+
Songs
Including arias, solo cantatas, etc., with or without obligato chorus or refrain
Orchestral, etc., accompaniment
Original compositions
Collections
Including miscellaneous collections
1611 Full scores
1612 Vocal scores with piano accompaniment
Separate works
Full scores
1613 Orchestral accompaniment
1613.3 Other accompaniment
Class here works with accompaniment of string orchestra, band, other ensemble of two or more instruments, or electronic accompaniment
For accompaniment of piano and one other instrument, see M1621.3
1614 Vocal scores with piano accompaniment
Arrangements
Collections
1615 Full scores
1616 Vocal scores with piano accompaniment
Separate works

Vocal music
  Secular vocal music
    Songs
      Orchestral, etc., accompaniment
        Arrangements
          Separate works -- Continued
1617 Full scores
  For accompaniment of piano and one other instrument, see M1621.3
1618 Vocal scores with piano accompaniment
      Piano accompaniment and unaccompanied
        Collections
          Two or more composers
1619 General
1619.5.A-Z Individual poets, A-Z
1620 One composer
        Separate works
1621 Piano accompaniment
1621.2 Unaccompanied
1621.3 Accompaniment of piano and one other instrument
1621.4 Song cycles
1622 Vaudeville, music-hall songs, etc.
  Class here songs published between 1850 and 1923
  For songs published before 1850, see M1621
  For songs published after 1923, see the country of origin under National music, M1628-M1853
      Accompaniment of one instrument other than piano
        Collections
          Plucked instrument
1623 General
1623.4 Harp
1623.5 Lute
1623.8 Other instrument
        Separate works
          Plucked instrument
1624 General
1624.4 Harp
1624.5 Lute
1624.7 Wind instrument
1624.8 Other instrument
    Recitations with music
      Including all solo vocalization not sung
      Class here secular and sacred works

Vocal music
Secular vocal music
Recitations with music -- Continued
1625 Accompaniment of orchestra or other ensemble
For sacred recitations with mixed chorus and orchestra or other ensemble, see M2020.3
For secular recitations with men's chorus and orchestra or other ensemble, see M1538.3
For secular recitations with mixed chorus and orchestra or other ensemble, see M1530.3
For secular recitations with treble chorus and orchestra or other ensemble, see M1543.3
1626 Accompaniment of piano or other instrument
Including piano scores
For piano-vocal scores of secular recitations with men's chorus, see M1540.3
For piano-vocal scores of secular recitations with mixed chorus, see M1533.3
For piano-vocal scores of secular recitations with treble chorus, see M1544.3
For vocal and chorus scores of sacred recitations with mixed chorus, see M2023.3
National music
Including solo songs, part-songs, collections of texts with the tunes indicated, and instrumental arrangements
Class here folk, national, ethnic, patriotic, political, popular music, etc.
For composers' settings of folk music and songs, see the class for the medium of performance, e.g., choruses, M1530-M1610; songs, M1611-M1626
International
1627 Collections
1627.15 Separate works
1627.5.A-Z Songs and music about famous persons. By person, A-Z
For persons in the United States, see M1659-M1659.5
North America
United States
1628 Songsters
Class here collections of songs generally without the music, but with indications of the tunes
Broadsides
Class here works with or without music
1628.2 Collections
1628.3 Separate works
1629 General collections
For collections of cowboy songs cataloged after 1997, see M1977.C6

Vocal music
Secular vocal music
National music
North America
United States -- Continued

1629.3.A-Z National holidays, A-Z
Class here collections and separate works
1629.3.A1 Two or more holidays
Armistice Day, see M1629.3.V4
1629.3.C5 Christmas
1629.3.C6 Columbus Day
1629.3.E3 Easter
1629.3.E5 Election Day
1629.3.F4 Flag Day
1629.3.F5 Fourth of July
1629.3.G8 Groundhog Day
Independence Day, see M1629.3.F5
1629.3.L3 Labor Day
1629.3.L5 Lincoln's Birthday
1629.3.M3 Memorial Day
1629.3.N4 New Year's Day
1629.3.S3 Saint Patrick's Day
1629.3.T4 Thanksgiving Day
1629.3.V4 Veterans Day
1629.3.W3 Washington's Birthday
1629.5 National songs, etc., combined in cantatas, etc., for patriotic occasions
Special collections
1629.6.A-Z By region, A-Z
1629.7.A-W By state, A-W (Table M1)
Cf. M1657, Collection of songs about states and cities
Cf. M1658.A+, Separate songs, by state
1630 Separate songs (General)
Popular music
1630.18 Collections
1630.2 Separate songs
1630.3.A-Z Special songs. By title, A-Z
1630.3.A5 America (My country 'tis of thee)
1630.3.A6 America the beautiful
1630.3.B3 Battle hymn of the Republic
1630.3.C6 Columbia the gem of the ocean
1630.3.D4 Dixie
1630.3.H3 Hail Columbia
1630.3.H6 Home, sweet home
Star-spangled banner
Class arrangements not specified below with the class for the medium of performance, e.g., M1258, band settings
1630.3.S68 The Anacreontic song
By date of edition

Vocal music
Secular vocal music
National music
North America
United States
Special songs. By title, A-Z
Star-spangled banner -- Continued

1630.3.S69 Broadsides
By date of edition

1630.3.S7 Song and part-song editions
By Muller number to 1864 (Joseph Muller, The Star spangled banner, 1935); then by date and initial if necessary

1630.3.S72 Piano, organ, etc., editions, with or without words
Class here editions for one or more pianos, two or more hands

1630.3.S74 Piano, organ, etc., variations, fantasies, etc.

1630.3.S76 Anacreontic parodies
Class here texts different from F.S. Key's

1630.3.S78 Other musical settings
Class here tunes different from the Anacreontic
Including J. Hewitt, The Star spangled banner, 1819

1630.3.Y2 Yankee Doodle

Special topics

1631 American Revolution, 1775-1783

1632 1783-1812

War of 1812

1633 Collections

1634 Separate songs

Mexican War, 1846-1848

1635 Collections

1636 Separate songs

Civil War, 1861-1865

General

1637 Collections

1638 Separate songs

(1638.2) Peace Jubilee, Boston
See M1642.2-M1642.3

Union

1639 Collections

1640 Separate songs

Confederate

1641 Collections

1642 Separate songs

Peace Jubilees, Boston

1642.2 National Peace Jubilee and Music Festival, 1869

Vocal music
Secular vocal music
National music
North America
United States
Special topics
Peace Jubilees, Boston -- Continued
1642.3 World's Peace Jubilee and International Musical Festival, 1872
Spanish-American War, 1898
1643 Collections
1644 Separate songs
1645 Relations with Mexico, 1914-1917
1646 World War, 1914-1918
World War, 1939-1945
1647 Before December 1941
1648 December 1941-1945
1649 Korean War, 1950-1953
1650 Vietnamese Conflict, 1961-1975
Songs about states and cities
1657 Collections
Cf. M1629.7.A+, Special collections, by state
Separate songs
1658.A-W By state, A-W (Table M1)
1658.5.A-Z By city, A-Z
1659.A-Z Presidents, statesmen, generals, etc. By person, A-Z
1659.5.A-Z Other famous persons. By person, A-Z
Political movement, party, campaign songs
1659.7 Collections
1659.8 Nonpartisan songs
Republican
1660 Collections
1661 Separate songs
Democratic
1662 Collections
1663 Separate songs
Other political parties, movements, etc., A-Z
Including labor organizations, etc.
1664.A-Z Collections
1664.A35 Abolitionist movement
1664.A5 American cooperative movement
1664.A55 American Independent Party
American Party, see M1664.K5
Anti-prohibition movement, see M1664.P82
1664.C6 Communist Party of the United States of America
1664.F15 Farmer-Labor Party
1664.F2 Farmers' Alliance (U.S.). National Farmers' Alliance and Industrial Union

Vocal music
Secular vocal music
National music
North America
United States
Special topics
Political movement, party, campaign songs
Other political parties, movements, etc., A-Z
Collections -- Continued

1664.F4 Federal Party (U.S.)
1664.F8 Free-Soil Party (U.S.)
1664.G8 Greenback Labor Party
1664.K5 Know-nothing Party. American Party
1664.K7 Ku-Klux Klan
1664.L3 Labor organizations
Class here songs of the American Federation of Labor (A.F.L.); Committee for Industrial Organization (C.I.O.); Industrial Workers of the World (I.W.W.); Knights of Labor; etc.
Cf. M1977.L3, Labor songs
1664.N3 National Recovery Administration
1664.P6 Populist Party (U.S.)
1664.P7 Progressive Party (1912)
Prohibition and anti-prohibition movements
1664.P8 Prohibition movement
1664.P82 Anti-prohibition movement
1664.S4 Single tax movement
1664.S67 Socialism
1664.T8 Townsend National Recovery Plan, Inc.
1664.W4 Whig Party (U.S.)
1664.W8 Woman's suffrage movement
1665.A-Z Separate works
1665.A35 Abolitionist movement
1665.A5 American cooperative movement
1665.A55 American Independent Party
American Party, see M1665.K5
Anti-prohibition movement, see M1665.P82
1665.C6 Communist Party of the United States of America
1665.F15 Farmer-Labor Party
1665.F2 Farmers' Alliance (U.S.). National Farmers' Alliance and Industrial Union
1665.F4 Federal Party (U.S.)
1665.F8 Free-Soil Party (U.S.)
1665.G8 Greenback Labor Party
1665.K5 Know-nothing Party. American Party
1665.K7 Ku-Klux Klan

Vocal music
Secular vocal music
National music
North America
United States
Special topics
Political movement, party, campaign songs
Other political parties, movements, etc., A-Z
Separate works -- Continued

1665.L3 Labor organizations
Class here songs of the American Federation of Labor (A.F.L.); Committee for Industrial Organization (C.I.O.); Industrial Workers of the World (I.W.W.); Knights of Labor; etc.
Cf. M1978.L3, Labor songs

1665.N3 National Recovery Administration
1665.P6 Populist Party (U.S.)
1665.P7 Progressive Party (1912)
Prohibition and anti-prohibition movements
1665.P8 Prohibition movement
1665.P82 Anti-prohibition movement
1665.S4 Single tax movement
1665.S67 Socialism
1665.T8 Townsend National Recovery Plan, Inc.
1665.W4 Whig Party (U.S.)
1665.W8 Woman's suffrage movement

Patriotic and other national songs arranged for piano
For the Star-spangled banner, see M1630.3.S72

1666 Collections
1667 Separate works

Ethnic music
1668 General
1668.1 British American
1668.2 Irish American
1668.3 German American
1668.4 Hispanic American
1668.6 Scandinavian American
1668.7 Slavic American
1668.8 French American
Including Cajun
1668.9.A-Z Other, A-Z
1669 Indian
Afro-American
Class here accompanied or unaccompanied vocal compositions, including spirituals

Vocal music
Secular vocal music
National music
North America
United States
Special topics
Ethnic music
Afro-American -- Continued
1670 Collections
1671 Separate songs
Territories, A-Z
1672.A-Z Collections
1672.C2 Canal Zone
1672.G8 Guam
Puerto Rico, see M1681.P6+
Samoa, American, see M1844.S2+
1672.V5 Virgin Islands
1673.A-Z Separate songs
1673.C2 Canal Zone
1673.G8 Guam
Puerto Rico, see M1681.P6+
Samoa, American, see M1844.S2+
1673.V5 Virgin Islands
1675.A-Z American songs on foreign wars, etc., in which the United States has not participated
e.g.
1675.R85 Russo-Japanese War, 1904-1905
1676.A-Z Patriotic societies and organizations, A-Z
1676.A1 General
American Legion and Auxiliary
1676.A5 American Legion
1676.A52 Auxiliary
1676.B5 Blue Star Mothers
1676.D3 Daughters of the American Revolution
1676.D4 Daughters of Union Veterans of the Civil War
1676.D45 Daughters of Utah Pioneers
1676.D5 Death Valley '49ers
1676.D6 Disabled American Veterans
1676.F5 Filipino Federation of America
1676.G6 Gold Star Mothers, American, Inc.
1676.G7 Grand Army of the Republic
1676.J4 Jewish War Veterans of the United States of America
1676.L97 Lyceum League
1676.M48 Military Order of the Loyal Legion of the United States
1676.M5 Military Order of the Purple Heart
1676.N3 National Guard Association of the United States
Order Sons of Italy in America, see M1676.S56

	Vocal music
	Secular vocal music
	National music
	North America
	United States
	Special topics
	Patriotic societies and organizations, A-Z -- Continued
1676.P3	Pershing Rifles
1676.Q3	Quarante hommes et huit chevaux, Société des (40 and 8)
1676.S54	Society of Mayflower Descendants
1676.S55	Society of the Cincinnati
1676.S56	Sons of Italy in America, Order
1676.S6	Sons of the American Revolution
1676.S7	Sons of Union Veterans of the Civil War
1676.T8	Transylvanians, Society of
1676.U6	Union League of America
1676.U7	United Daughters of the Confederacy
1676.U77	United Service Organizations (U.S.) (USO)
	Veterans of Foreign Wars of the United States and Ladies' Auxiliary
1676.V4	Veterans of Foreign Wars of the United States
1676.V42	Ladies' Auxiliary
1677	Old folks concerts of Father Kemp
1677.2.A-Z	Exhibitions. By place, A-Z, and date
1677.2.C3 1893	Chicago. World's Columbian Exposition
1677.2.C3 1933	Chicago. Century of Progress International Exposition
1677.2.C3 1948	Chicago. Railroad Fair
1677.2.C6 1936	Cleveland. Great Lakes Exposition
1677.2.M65 1967	Montreal. Expo 67
1677.2.N4 1939	New York. World's Fair
1677.2.P4 1876	Philadelphia. Centennial Exhibition
1677.2.S25 1904	St. Louis. Louisiana Purchase Exposition
1677.2.S28 1968	San Antonio. Hemisfair
1677.2.S3 1915	San Diego. Panama-California Exposition
1677.2.S4 1939	San Francisco. Golden Gate International Exposition
1677.2.S65 1974	Spokane. Expo 74
1677.3.A-Z	Patriotic monuments, dedicatory exercises, etc. By place, A-Z
1677.4	American Revolution Bicentennial, 1776-1976
1677.8	Other topics
	Canada
	General
1678	Collections
1679	Separate works
	Popular music
1679.18	Collections
1679.2	Separate works
	North and South America

Vocal music
Secular vocal music
National music
North and South America -- Continued
1680 General
Popular music
Including music published in the United States in Spanish for distribution in other countries
1680.18 Collections
1680.2 Separate works
West Indies
1681.A1 General
1681.A5-Z By island, country, etc., A-Z
e.g.
Netherlands Antilles
1681.N48 General
Popular music
1681.N4818 Collections
1681.N482 Separate works
Puerto Rico
1681.P6 General
Popular music
1681.P618 Collections
1681.P62 Separate works
Bermuda
1681.5 General
Popular music
1681.518 Collections
1681.52 Separate works
Mexico
General
1682 Collections
1683 Separate works
Popular music
1683.18 Collections
1683.2 Separate works
Central America
General
1684.A-Z Collections
1684.A1 General
1684.A5-Z By region or country, A-Z
1684.C6 Costa Rica
1684.G9 Guatemala
1684.H5 Honduras
1684.N4 Nicaragua
1684.P2 Panama
1684.S2 El Salvador
1685.A-Z Separate works. By region or country, A-Z
1685.A1 General
1685.C6 Costa Rica
1685.G9 Guatemala
1685.H5 Honduras

Vocal music
Secular vocal music
National music
Central America
Separate works
By region or country, A-Z -- Continued
1685.N4 Nicaragua
1685.P2 Panama
1685.S2 El Salvador
Popular music
For popular music, add to the Cutter for the region or country as follows:
.x18 *Collections*
.x2 *Separate works*
South America
1686 General
By region or country, A-Z
Subclasses for individual countries continue at M1688
General
1687.A-Z Collections
1687.A7 Argentina
1687.B6 Bolivia
Brazil, see M1689+
British Guyana, see M1687.G9
Chile, see M1691+
1687.C6 Colombia
1687.E2 Ecuador
1687.G9 Guyana
1687.P2 Paraguay
Peru, see M1693+
1687.S9 Surinam
1687.U6 Uruguay
1687.V3 Venezuela
1688.A-Z Separate works
Subclasses for individual countries begin at M1687
1688.A7 Argentina
1688.B6 Bolivia
British Guyana, see M1688.G9, M1689+
Chile, see M1691+
1688.C6 Colombia
1688.E2 Ecuador
1688.G9 Guyana
1688.P2 Paraguay
Peru, see M1693+
1688.S9 Surinam
1688.U6 Uruguay
1688.V3 Venezuela

Vocal music
Secular vocal music
National music
South America
By region or country, A-Z -- Continued
Popular music
For popular music, add to the Cutter for the region or country as follows
.x18 *Collections*
.x2 *Separate works*
Brazil
General
1689 Collections
1690 Separate works
Popular music
1690.18 Collections
1690.2 Separate works
Chile
General
1691 Collections
1692 Separate works
Popular music
1692.18 Collections
1692.2 Separate works
Peru
General
1693 Collections
1694 Separate works
Popular music
1694.18 Collections
1694.2 Separate works
Europe
1698 General
Austria
General
1702 Collections
1703 Separate works
Popular music
1703.18 Collections
1703.2 Separate works
Czechoslovakia. Czech Republic
General
1704 Collections
1705 Separate works
Popular music
1705.18 Collections
1705.2 Separate works
Hungary
General
1706 Collections
1707 Separate works
Popular music
1707.18 Collections

Vocal music
Secular vocal music
National music
Europe
Hungary
Popular music -- Continued
1707.2 Separate works
Slovakia
General
1708 Collections
1709 Separate works
Popular music
1709.18 Collections
1709.2 Separate works
Balkan Peninsula
Bulgaria
General
1712 Collections
1713 Separate works
Popular music
1713.18 Collections
1713.2 Separate works
Greece
General
1714 Collections
1715 Separate works
Popular music
1715.18 Collections
1715.2 Separate works
Romania
General
1718 Collections
1719 Separate works
Popular music
1719.18 Collections
1719.2 Separate works
Yugoslavia
General
1720 Collections
1721 Separate works
Popular music
1721.18 Collections
1721.2 Separate works
Slovenia
General
1721.3 Collections
1721.4 Separate works
Popular music
1721.5 Collections
1721.6 Separate works
Croatia
General
1722.3 Collections

Vocal music
Secular vocal music
National music
Europe
Balkan Peninsula
Croatia
General -- Continued
1722.4 Separate works
Popular music
1722.5 Collections
1722.6 Separate works
Bosnia and Hercegovina
General
1723.3 Collections
1723.4 Separate works
Popular music
1723.5 Collections
1723.6 Separate works
Albania
General
1724 Collections
1725 Separate works
Popular music
1725.18 Collections
1725.2 Separate works
Macedonia (Republic)
General
1725.3 Collections
1725.4 Separate works
Popular music
1725.5 Collections
1725.6 Separate works
Belgium
General
1726 Collections
1727 Separate works
Popular music
1727.18 Collections
1727.2 Separate works
Local, A-Z
1728.A-Z Collections
1729.A-Z Separate works
Finland
General
1729.3 Collections
1729.4 Separate works
Popular music
1729.5 Collections
1729.6 Separate works
France
General
1730 Collections
1731 Separate works

Vocal music
Secular vocal music
National music
Europe
France -- Continued
Popular music
1731.18 Collections
1731.2 Separate works
Local, A-Z
1732.A-Z Collections
1733.A-Z Separate works
Germany
General
1734 Collections
1735 Separate works
Popular music
1735.18 Collections
1735.2 Separate works
Local, A-Z
1736.A-Z Collections
1737.A-Z Separate works
British Isles
General
1738 Collections
1739 Separate works
Popular music
1739.18 Collections
1739.2 Separate works
1739.3 Broadsides
England
General
1740 Collections
1741 Separate works
Popular music
1741.18 Collections
1741.2 Separate works
Wales
General
1742 Collections
1743 Separate works
Popular music
1743.18 Collections
1743.2 Separate works
Ireland
General
1744 Collections
1745 Separate works
Popular music
1745.18 Collections
1745.2 Separate works
Northern Ireland
General
1745.3 Collections

Vocal music
Secular vocal music
National music
Europe
British Isles
Northern Ireland
General -- Continued
1745.4 Separate works
Popular music
1745.5 Collections
1745.6 Separate works
Scotland
General
1746 Collections
1747 Separate works
Popular music
1747.18 Collections
1747.2 Separate works
Italy
General
1748 Collections
1749 Separate works
Popular music
1749.18 Collections
1749.2 Separate works
Local, A-Z
1750.A-Z Collections
1751.A-Z Separate works
Netherlands
General
1752 Collections
1753 Separate works
Popular music
1753.18 Collections
1753.2 Separate works
Local, A-Z
1754.A-Z Collections
1755.A-Z Separate works
Poland
General
1755.3 Collections
1755.4 Separate works
Popular music
1755.5 Collections
1755.6 Separate works
Russia. Soviet Union. Russia (Federation)
For former Soviet republics in Asia, see M1795+
General
1756 Collections
1757 Separate works
Popular music
1757.18 Collections

Vocal music
Secular vocal music
National music
Europe
Russia. Soviet Union. Russia (Federation)
Popular music -- Continued
1757.2 Separate works
Latvia
General
1758 Collections
1759 Separate works
Popular music
1759.18 Collections
1759.2 Separate works
Ukraine
General
1764 Collections
1765 Separate works
Popular music
1765.18 Collections
1765.2 Separate works
1766.A-Z Other former Soviet republics (Europe), A-Z
Subclasses for individual countries continue at M1767
Belarus
General
1766.B4 Collections
Estonia
General
1766.E6 Collections
Lithuania
General
1766.L4 Collections
Moldova
General
1766.M5 Collections
1767.A-Z Other former Soviet republics (Europe), A-Z
Subclasses for individual countries begin at M1766
Belarus
General
1767.B4 Separate works
Popular music
1767.B418 Collections
1767.B42 Separate works
Estonia
General
1767.E6 Separate works
Popular music
1767.E618 Collections
1767.E62 Separate works
Lithuania
General

Vocal music
Secular vocal music
National music
Europe
Other former Soviet republics (Europe), A-Z
Lithuania
General -- Continued
1767.L4 Separate works
Popular music
1767.L418 Collections
1767.L42 Separate works
Moldova
General
1767.M5 Separate works
Popular music
1767.M518 Collections
1767.M52 Separate works
Scandinavia
General
1768 Collections
1769 Separate works
Popular music
1769.18 Collections
1769.2 Separate works
Denmark
General
1770 Collections
1771 Separate works
Popular music
1771.18 Collections
1771.2 Separate works
Iceland
General
1771.3 Collections
1771.4 Separate works
Popular music
1771.5 Collections
1771.6 Separate works
Norway
General
1772 Collections
1773 Separate works
Popular music
1773.18 Collections
1773.2 Separate works
Sweden
General
1774 Collections
1775 Separate works
Popular music
1775.18 Collections
1775.2 Separate works
Greenland

Vocal music
Secular vocal music
National music
Europe
Scandinavia
Greenland -- Continued
General
1776 Collections
1777 Separate works
Popular music
1777.18 Collections
1777.2 Separate works
Spain
General
1779 Collections
1780 Separate works
Popular music
1780.18 Collections
1780.2 Separate works
Portugal
General
1781 Collections
1782 Separate works
Popular music
1782.18 Collections
1782.2 Separate works
Switzerland
General
1784 Collections
1785 Separate works
Popular music
1785.18 Collections
1785.2 Separate works
Local, A-Z
1786.A-Z Collections
1787.A-Z Separate works
1788.A-1789.Z Other European countries, A-Z
Subclasses for individual countries continue at M1789
Liechtenstein
General
1788.L76 Collections
Luxembourg
General
1788.L8 Collections
Malta
General
1788.M43 Collections
Monaco
General
1788.M63 Collections

Vocal music
Secular vocal music
National music
Europe -- Continued

1789.A-Z Other European countries, A-Z
Subclasses for individual countries begin at M1788
Liechtenstein
General
1789.L56 Separate works
Popular music
1789.L5618 Collections
1789.L562 Separate works
Luxembourg
General
1789.L8 Separate works
Popular music
1789.L818 Collections
1789.L82 Separate works
Malta
General
1789.M3 Separate works
Popular music
1789.M318 Collections
1789.M32 Separate works
Monaco
General
1789.M6 Separate works
Popular music
1789.M618 Collections
1789.M62 Separate works
Asia
1795 General
Cf. M1828, General collections of music from the Arab countries
Saudi Arabia
General
1797 Collections
1798 Separate works
Popular music
1798.18 Collections
1798.2 Separate works
Armenia
General
1800 Collections
1801 Separate works
Popular music
1801.18 Collections
1801.2 Separate works

Vocal music
Secular vocal music
National music
Asia -- Continued
China
For general collections of the music of Tibet, see M1824.T5+
For general separate works and popular music of Tibet, see M1825.T5+
General
1804 Collections
1805 Separate works
Popular music
1805.18 Collections
1805.2 Separate works
Chinese operas
Including Beijing opera
1805.3 General
1805.4.A-Z Local types and styles. By region, A-Z
Taiwan
General
1806 Collections
1807 Separate works
Popular music
1807.18 Collections
1807.2 Separate works
India
General
1808 Collections
1809 Separate works
Popular music
1809.18 Collections
1809.2 Separate works
Israel. Palestine
Cf. M1850+, Jews
General
1810 Collections
1811 Separate works
Popular music
1811.18 Collections
1811.2 Separate works
Japan
General
1812 Collections
1813 Separate works
Popular music
1813.18 Collections
1813.2 Separate works
Korea
Including South Korea
General
1816 Collections
1817 Separate works

Vocal music
Secular vocal music
National music
Asia
Korea -- Continued
Popular music
1817.18 Collections
1817.2 Separate works
Korea (North)
General
1818 Collections
1819 Separate works
Popular music
1819.18 Collections
1819.2 Separate works
1819.3 Revolutionary operas
Iran
General
1820 Collections
1821 Separate works
Popular music
1821.18 Collections
1821.2 Separate works
Philippines
General
1822 Collections
1823 Separate works
Popular music
1823.18 Collections
1823.2 Separate works
1824-1825 Other regions or countries, A-Z
Subclasses for individual regions and countries continue at M1825
e.g.
Azerbaijan
General
1824.A9 Collections
Cyprus
General
1824.C9 Collections
Georgia
General
1824.G45 Collections
Tibet
General
1824.T5 Collections
Turkey
General
1824.T8 Collections
1825.A-Z Other regions or countries, A-Z
Subclasses for individual regions and countries begin at M1824
e.g.

Vocal music
Secular vocal music
National music
Asia
Other regions or countries, A-Z -- Continued
Azerbaijan
General
1825.A98 Separate works
Popular music
1825.A9818 Collections
1825.A982 Separate works
Cyprus
General
1825.C9 Separate works
Popular music
1825.C918 Collections
1825.C92 Separate works
Georgia
General
1825.G28 Separate works
Popular music
1825.G2818 Collections
1825.G282 Separate works
Tibet
General
1825.T5 Separate works
Popular music
1825.T518 Collections
1825.T52 Separate works
Turkey
General
1825.T8 Separate works
Popular music
1825.T818 Collections
1825.T82 Separate works
1828 Arab countries
Class here general collections of music from the Arab world
For music of individual Arab countries of Africa, see M1838.A+
For music of individual Arab countries of Asia, see M1824+
For music of Saudi Arabia, see M1797+
Africa
1830 General
1831.A-Z By ethnic group, A-Z
Class here music of individual Black African ethnic groups; for music of two or more groups published together, see General or the country; for music of White African groups, see the country, e.g., Afrikaners, see South Africa
By country

Vocal music
Secular vocal music
National music
Africa
By country -- Continued
South Africa
1834 General
Popular music
1834.18 Collections
1834.2 Separate works
1838.A-Z Other, A-Z
Subarrange each country as follows:
General
Popular music
For popular music of individual countries, add to the Cutter number for the country as follows, as for Algeria below:
.x18 Collections
.x2 Separate works
Algeria
1838.A4 General
Popular music
1838.A418 Collections
1838.A42 Separate works
Australia
General
1840 Collections
1841 Separate works
Popular music
1841.18 Collections
1841.2 Separate works
New Zealand
General
1842 Collections
1843 Separate works
Popular music
1843.18 Collections
1843.2 Separate works
Pacific Islands
1844.A1 General
By island or group, A-Z
Subarrange each island or group as follows:
1844.A5-Z General
Popular music
For popular music of individual islands or groups, add to the Cutter number for the island or group as follows, as for Samoa below:
.x18 Collections
.x2 Separate works
Samoa
1844.S2 General

Vocal music
Secular vocal music
National music
Pacific Islands
By island or group, A-Z
Samoa -- Continued
Popular music
1844.S218 Collections
1844.S22 Separate works
Indian Ocean islands
1846.A1 General
By island, A-Z
Subarrange each island as follows:
1846.A5-Z General
Popular music
For popular music of individual islands, add to the Cutter number for the island as follows, as for Mauritius below:
.x18 Collections
.x2 Separate works
Mauritius
1846.M4 General
Popular music
1846.M418 Collections
1846.M42 Separate works
Jews
Cf. M1810+, Israel. Palestine
1850 General
1851 Zionist, Hasidic, and other movements
By language
1852 Yiddish
1853 Other dialects
Songs (part and solo) of special character
For political songs, see M1627+
Fraternal society songs
Class here sacred and secular songs
Freemason
American publications
Collections
1900.M3 General
1900.M31 Blue Lodge
1900.M32 Chapter
1900.M35 Commandery
1900.M37 Scottish Rite (Masonic order)
1900.M38 Mystic Order of Veiled Prophets of the Enchanted Realm
1900.M4 Mystic Shrine. Ancient Arabic Order of the Nobles of the Mystic Shrine for North America
1900.M41 DeMolay for Boys
1900.M42 Ancient Egyptian Order of Scioto
Eastern Star, see M1905.E3
Rainbow, Order of, for Girls, see M1905.R3

Vocal music
Secular vocal music
Songs (part and solo) of special character
Fraternal society songs
Freemason
American publications -- Continued
Separate works
1901.M3 General
1901.M31 Blue Lodge
1901.M32 Chapter
1901.M35 Commandery
1901.M37 Scottish Rite (Masonic order)
1901.M38 Mystic Order of Veiled Prophets of the Enchanted Realm
1901.M4 Mystic Shrine. Ancient Arabic Order of the Nobles of the Mystic Shrine for North America
1901.M41 DeMolay for Boys
1901.M42 Ancient Egyptian Order of Scioto
Eastern Star, Order of, see M1906.E3
Rainbow for Girls, see M1906.R3
Other fraternal societies
American publications
Collections
1905.A1 General
1905.A46 Alhambra, Order of
1905.A55 Amaranth, Order of
1905.B5 B'nai B'rith
1905.D5 Deutscher Orden der Harugari (German Order of Harugari)
1905.E2 Eagles, Fraternal Order of
1905.E3 Eastern Star, Order of
1905.E5 Elks, Benevolent and Protective Order of
German Order of Harugari, see M1905.D5
Grange, see M1905.P3
1905.J6 Job's Daughters, International Order of
1905.K5 Knights of Columbus
1905.K54 Knights of Malta
1905.K55 Knights of Pythias
1905.K6 Knights of the Golden Eagle
Modern Woodmen of America, see M1905.W7
1905.M7 Moose, Loyal Order of
National Grange, see M1905.P3
1905.O3 Odd-Fellows, Independent Order of
1905.P2 P.E.O. Sisterhood
1905.P3 Patrons of Husbandry. National Grange
1905.R3 Rainbow, Order of, for Girls
1905.R33 Rebekah Assemblies, International Association of, IOOF
1905.W6 Woman's Benefit Association of the Maccabees

Vocal music
Secular vocal music
Songs (part and solo) of special character
Fraternal society songs
Other fraternal societies
American publications
Collections -- Continued

1905.W7 Supreme Forest Woodmen Circle (U.S.), Modern Woodmen of America, and other foresters' fraternal organizations

Separate works

1906.A46 Alhambra, Order of
1906.A55 Amaranth, Order of
1906.B5 B'nai B'rith
1906.D5 Deutscher Orden der Harugari (German Order of Harugari)
1906.E2 Eagles, Fraternal Order of
1906.E3 Eastern Star, Order of
1906.E5 Elks, Benevolent and Protective Order of
German Order of Harugari, see M1906.D5
Grange, see M1906.P3
1906.J6 Job's Daughters, International Order of
1906.K5 Knights of Columbus
1906.K54 Knights of Malta
1906.K55 Knights of Pythias
1906.K6 Knights of the Golden Eagle
Modern Woodman of America, see M1906.W7
1906.M7 Moose, Loyal Order of
National Grange, see M1906.P3
1906.O3 Odd-Fellows, Independent Order of
1906.P2 P.E.O. Sisterhood
1906.P3 Patrons of Husbandry. National Grange
1906.R3 Rainbow, Order of, for Girls
1906.R33 Rebekah Assemblies, International Association of, IOOF
1906.W6 Woman's Benefit Association of the Maccabees
1906.W7 Supreme Forest Woodmen Circle (U.S.), Modern Woodmen of America, and other foresters' fraternal organizations

Other societies, organizations, and clubs, A-Z
Cf. M1676.A+, National music
Cf. M1977+, Songs (part and solo) by topic

1920.A-Z Collections
e.g.
1920.A35 Alcoholics Anonymous
1920.I55 International Business Machines Corporation
1920.N13 National Federation of Music Clubs
1920.P2 National PTA (U.S.)
1920.R6 Rotary clubs. Rotary International

Vocal music
Secular vocal music
Songs (part and solo) of special character
Society songs, secular and sacred
Other societies, organizations, and clubs, A-Z
Collections -- Continued
1920.S54 Society for the Preservation and Encouragement of Barber Shop Quartet Singing in America
1920.U48 United Nations. Children's Fund
1921.A-Z Separate works
e.g.
1921.A35 Alcoholics Anonymous
1921.I55 International Business Machines Corporation
1921.N13 National Federation of Music Clubs
1921.P2 National PTA (U.S.)
1921.R6 Rotary clubs. Rotary International
1921.S54 Society for the Preservation and Encouragement of Barber Shop Quartet Singing in America
1921.U48 United Nations. Children's Fund
Students' songs
Class here college and university songs
For songs of primary and secondary schools, see M1992+
International
1940 Collections
1941 Separate works
United States
1945 Miscellaneous collections
Men's colleges and universities
Collections
1946 Miscellaneous
1948.A-Z Individual institutions. By name, A-Z
1950.A-Z Separate songs. By name of institution, A-Z
Women's colleges and universities
Collections
1952 Miscellaneous
1954.A-Z Individual institutions. By name, A-Z
1956.A-Z Separate songs. By name of institution, A-Z
Coeducational colleges and universities
Collections
1957 Miscellaneous
1958.A-Z Individual institutions. By name, A-Z
1959.A-Z Separate songs. By name of institution, A-Z
1960.A-Z Fraternities, sororities, A-Z
Other countries
1961 Austria. Hungary. Germany. Switzerland
1962 France. Belgium
1964 Great Britain. Ireland
1966 Netherlands
1967 Italy. Spain. Portugal

Vocal music
Secular vocal music
Songs (part and solo) of special character
Students' songs
Other countries -- Continued

1970 Canada
1972 Russia. Soviet Union. Russia (Federation)
1973.A-Z Other, A-Z

By topic, A-Z

1977.A-Z Collections
1977.A4 Aeronautics. Aviation
Aged, see M1977.S45
1977.A6 Animals
1977.A65 Antiques
Archery, see M1977.S705
1977.A7 Artists
1977.A8 Atoms
Automobile racing, see M1977.S707
Autumn, see M1977.S413
Aviation, see M1977.A4
1977.B3 Balloons
Baseball, see M1977.S713
Basketball, see M1977.S714
1977.B38 Bawdy songs
1977.B4 Beauticians
1977.B5 Birds
1977.B53 Birthdays
Bowling, see M1977.S715
Boxing, see M1977.S716
1977.B6 Boy Scouts of America, Camp Fire Girls, Girl Scouts of the United States of America, Wandervögel, etc.
1977.B7 Brotherhood Week
1977.B8 Bullfights
Camp Fire Girls, see M1977.B6
1977.C3 Camping
1977.C34 Canals
Cars (Automobiles), see M1977.M6
1977.C4 Cemeteries
1977.C43 Chemistry
1977.C45 Circus
1977.C46 Civil defense
1977.C47 Civil rights
Comic songs, see M1977.H7
1977.C48 Communism
1977.C5 Community
Conduct of life, see M1977.M55
1977.C53 Conservation. Ecology. Pollution
1977.C55 Convicts. Prisoners. Ex-convicts

Vocal music
Secular vocal music
Songs (part and solo) of special character
By topic, A-Z
Collections -- Continued

1977.C6 Cowboy songs
For cowboy songs cataloged before 1998, see M1627-M1627.15, M1630, M1630.18-M1630.2, M1678-M1679.2, M1680-M1694.2, etc.
1977.C7 Crime. Criminals
Cycling, see M1977.S7165
1977.D4 Democracy
1977.D7 Drinking songs
Ecology, see M1977.C53
1977.E3 Economic conditions
1977.E33 Education
1977.E68 Emigration. Immigration
1977.E7 Epicures. Gourmets
Ethics, see M1977.M55
Ex-convicts, see M1977.C55
1977.F2 Farmers
1977.F26 Fathers
1977.F38 Fire prevention
1977.F4 Fire fighters
1977.F5 Fishers
1977.F54 Flowers
Football, see M1977.S718
1977.F6 Foresters. Forest fires
1977.G3 Gambling
1977.G38 Gays
1977.G46 Geography
Girl Scouts of the United States of America, see M1977.B6
Golf, see M1977.S72
Gourmets, see M1977.E7
1977.G9 Gymnastics
1977.H3 Halloween
1977.H4 Health
1977.H5 Hiking
1977.H58 Hobbies
1977.H6 Hoboes. Tramps
1977.H65 Homemakers. Housewives
Horse racing, see M1977.S723
Horsemanship, see M1977.S722
Housewives, see M1977.H65
1977.H7 Humorous songs
1977.H77 Hunger
1977.H8 Hunting
1977.H85 Husbands
Immigration, see M1977.E68
Income tax, see M1977.T3
1977.I5 Insurance salespeople

Vocal music
Secular vocal music
Songs (part and solo) of special character
By topic, A-Z
Collections -- Continued

1977.J7 Junior Republics
1977.J87 Juvenile delinquency
1977.L3 Labor
Cf. M1664+, songs of labor organizations in the United States
1977.L55 Littering
1977.L8 Lumbermen
1977.M3 Mail carriers
1977.M37 May Day
1977.M4 Medicine
1977.M44 Men
1977.M5 Miners
Missiles, see M1977.S63
1977.M54 Months
1977.M55 Morals. Ethics. Conduct of life
1977.M57 Mothers
1977.M6 Motor transportation. Transportation, Automotive
1977.M63 Mountaineering
1977.M8 Music publishing
1977.M83 Musicians
1977.N38 Nature
1977.N48 Newspaper carriers
1977.N5 Newspapers
1977.N8 Nurses
1977.N83 Nutrition
1977.O5 Olympics
1977.P4 Peace
1977.P45 Phonograph
1977.P47 Photography
1977.P5 Physical fitness
1977.P7 Police
Pollution, see M1977.C53
Postmen, see M1977.M3
1977.P74 Printing
Prisoners, see M1977.C55
1977.P75 Protest songs
1977.P8 Psychoanalysis
1977.R2 Radio. Television
1977.R3 Railroads
Rockets (Aeronautics), see M1977.S63
Rodeos, see M1977.S726
1977.S15 Safety songs
1977.S2 Sailors. Sea songs
1977.S25 Saint Valentine's Day
1977.S3 Science
Sea songs, see M1977.S2

Vocal music
Secular vocal music
Songs (part and solo) of special character
By topic, A-Z
Collections -- Continued
Seasons
1977.S4 General
1977.S413 Autumn
1977.S417 Spring
1977.S418 Summer
1977.S42 Winter
1977.S43 Secretaries
1977.S45 Senior citizens. Aged
1977.S48 Shepherds
1977.S5 Singing commercials
Skiing, see M1977.S727
Skydiving, see M1977.S73
1977.S55 Smoking
Soccer, see M1977.S75
1977.S6 Soldiers
1977.S63 Space (missiles, rockets, etc.)
Sports
1977.S7 General
1977.S705 Archery
1977.S707 Automobile racing
1977.S713 Baseball
1977.S714 Basketball
1977.S715 Bowling
1977.S716 Boxing
1977.S7165 Cycling
1977.S718 Football
1977.S72 Golf
1977.S722 Horsemanship
1977.S723 Horse racing
1977.S726 Rodeos
1977.S727 Skiing
1977.S73 Skydiving
1977.S75 Soccer
Spring, see M1977.S417
Summer, see M1977.S418
1977.T25 Tailors. Tailoring
1977.T3 Taxation
Television, see M1977.R2
1977.T55 Titanic (Steamship)
1977.T6 Toleration
Tramps, see M1977.H6
1977.T8 Travel
1977.T87 Truck drivers
(1977.T9) Turners
See M1977.G9
1977.T97 Typing (Writing)
Valentine's Day, see M1977.S25
1977.V5 Voting

Vocal music
Secular vocal music
Songs (part and solo) of special character
By topic, A-Z
Collections -- Continued

1977.W3 Waiters
Wandervögel, see M1977.B6
1977.W38 Weather
1977.W4 Weddings
1977.W54 Wine
Winter, see M1977.S42
1977.W57 Witchcraft
1977.W64 Women
Work, see M1977.L3
1977.Z6 Zodiac
1978.A-Z Separate works
1978.A4 Aeronautics. Aviation
Aged, see M1978.S45
1978.A6 Animals
1978.A65 Antiques
Archery, see M1978.S705
1978.A7 Artists
1978.A8 Atoms
Automobile racing, see M1978.S707
Autumn, see M1978.S413
Aviation, see M1978.A4
1978.B3 Balloons
Baseball, see M1978.S713
Basketball, see M1978.S714
1978.B38 Bawdy songs
1978.B4 Beauticians
1978.B5 Birds
1978.B53 Birthdays
Bowling, see M1978.S715
Boxing, see M1978.S716
1978.B6 Boy Scouts of America, Camp Fire Girls, Girl Scouts of the United States of America, Wandervögel, etc.
1978.B7 Brotherhood Week
1978.B8 Bullfights
Camp Fire Girls, see M1978.B6
1978.C3 Camping
1978.C34 Canals
Cars (Automobiles), see M1978.M6
1978.C4 Cemeteries
1978.C43 Chemistry
1978.C45 Circus
1978.C46 Civil defense
1978.C47 Civil rights
Comic songs, see M1978.H7
1978.C48 Communism
1978.C5 Community
Conduct of life, see M1978.M55

Vocal music
Secular vocal music
Songs (part and solo) of special character
By topic, A-Z
Separate works -- Continued

1978.C53 Conservation. Ecology. Pollution
1978.C55 Convicts. Prisoners. Ex-convicts
1978.C6 Cowboy songs
For cowboy songs cataloged before 1998, see M1627-M1627.15, M1630, M1630.18-M1630.2, M1678-M1679.2, M1680-M1694.2, etc.
1978.C7 Crime. Criminals
Cycling, see M1978.S7165
1978.D4 Democracy
1978.D7 Drinking songs
Ecology, see M1978.C53
1978.E3 Economic conditions
1978.E33 Education
1978.E68 Emigration. Immigration
1978.E7 Epicures. Gourmets
Ethics, see M1978.M55
Ex-convicts, see M1978.C55
1978.F2 Farmers
1978.F26 Fathers
1978.F38 Fire prevention
1978.F4 Fire fighters
1978.F5 Fishers
1978.F54 Flowers
Football, see M1978.S718
1978.F6 Foresters. Forest fires
1978.G3 Gambling
1978.G38 Gays
1978.G46 Geography
Girl Scouts of the United States of America, see M1978.B6
Golf, see M1978.S72
Gourmets, see M1978.E7
1978.G9 Gymnastics
1978.H3 Halloween
1978.H4 Health
1978.H5 Hiking
1978.H58 Hobbies
1978.H6 Hoboes. Tramps
1978.H65 Homemakers. Housewives
Horse racing, see M1978.S723
Horsemanship, see M1978.S722
Housewives, see M1978.H65
1978.H7 Humorous songs
1978.H77 Hunger
1978.H8 Hunting
1978.H85 Husbands
Immigration, see M1978.E68

Vocal music
Secular vocal music
Songs (part and solo) of special character
By topic, A-Z
Separate works -- Continued

Income tax, see M1978.T3
1978.I5 Insurance salespeople
1978.J7 Junior Republics
1978.J87 Juvenile delinquency
1978.L3 Labor
Cf. M1664+, songs of labor organizations in the United States
1978.L55 Littering
1978.L8 Lumbermen
1978.M3 Mail carriers
1978.M37 May Day
1978.M4 Medicine
1978.M44 Men
1978.M5 Miners
Missiles, see M1978.S63
1978.M54 Months
1978.M55 Morals. Ethics. Conduct of life
1978.M57 Mothers
1978.M6 Motor transportation. Transportation, Automotive
1978.M63 Mountaineering
1978.M8 Music publishing
1978.M83 Musicians
1978.N38 Nature
1978.N48 Newspaper carriers
1978.N5 Newspapers
1978.N8 Nurses
1978.N83 Nutrition
1978.O5 Olympics
1978.P4 Peace
1978.P45 Phonograph
1978.P47 Photography
1978.P5 Physical fitness
1978.P7 Police
Pollution, see M1978.C53
Postmen, see M1978.M3
1978.P74 Printing
Prisoners, see M1978.C55
1978.P75 Protest songs
1978.P8 Psychoanalysis
1978.R2 Radio. Television
1978.R3 Railroads
Rockets (Aeronautics), see M1978.S63
Rodeos, see M1978.S726
1978.S15 Safety songs
1978.S2 Sailors. Sea songs
1978.S25 Saint Valentine's Day
1978.S3 Science

Vocal music
Secular vocal music
songs (part and solo) of special character
By topic, A-Z
Separate works -- Continued
Sea songs, see M1978.S2
Seasons
1978.S4 General
1978.S413 Autumn
1978.S417 Spring
1978.S418 Summer
1978.S42 Winter
1978.S43 Secretaries
1978.S45 Senior citizens. Aged
1978.S48 Shepherds
1978.S5 Singing commercials
Skiing, see M1978.S727
Skydiving, see M1978.S73
1978.S55 Smoking
Soccer, see M1978.S75
1978.S6 Soldiers
1978.S63 Space (missiles, rockets, etc.)
Sports
1978.S7 General
1978.S705 Archery
1978.S707 Automobile racing
1978.S713 Baseball
1978.S714 Basketball
1978.S715 Bowling
1978.S716 Boxing
1978.S7165 Cycling
1978.S718 Football
1978.S72 Golf
1978.S722 Horsemanship
1978.S723 Horse racing
1978.S726 Rodeos
1978.S727 Skiing
1978.S73 Skydiving
1978.S75 Soccer
Spring, see M1978.S417
Summer, see M1978.S418
1978.T25 Tailors. Tailoring
1978.T3 Taxation
Television, see M1978.R2
1978.T55 Titanic (Steamship)
1978.T6 Toleration
Tramps, see M1978.H6
1978.T8 Travel
1978.T87 Truck drivers
(1978.T9) Turners
See M1978.G9
1978.T97 Typing (Writing)
Valentine's Day, see M1978.S25

Vocal music
Secular vocal music
Songs (part and solo) of special character
By topic, A-Z
Separate works -- Continued
1978.V5 Voting
1978.W3 Waiters
Wandervögel, see M1978.B6
1978.W38 Weather
1978.W4 Weddings
1978.W54 Wine
Winter, see M1978.S42
1978.W57 Witchcraft
1978.W64 Women
Work, see M1978.L3
1978.Z6 Zodiac
1985 Musical games
Cf. M1993, Action songs, drill songs, and musical games for children
Secular music for children
For children's picture books illustrating the lyrics of single songs, with or without the music, see PZ4.2+
1990 Kindergarten
Primary and secondary schools
1992 Miscellaneous collections
1993 Action songs. Drill songs. Musical games
Cf. M1985, Musical games
1994 School songbooks
School songs of particular schools. By school, A-Z
1994.5.A-Z Collections
1994.6.A-Z Separate songs
1995 Dramatic music
1996 Cantatas
Choruses, songs, etc.
For choruses with accompaniment of orchestra or other ensemble, see M1546.5
1997 Collections
For Boy Scouts of America, Girl Scouts of the United States of America, etc., see M1977.B6
1998 Separate works
For Boy Scouts of America, Girl Scouts of the United States of America, etc., see M1978.B6
Sacred vocal music
1999 Collections
Class here miscellaneous collections of sacred vocal music by two or more composers
For miscellaneous collections of sacred vocal works by one composer, see M3.1

Vocal music
Sacred vocal music -- Continued
Oratorios
Including works that may be staged
2000 Full scores
2002 Vocal and chorus scores without accompaniment
2003 Vocal scores with piano or organ accompaniment
Excerpts
2004 Original accompaniment
Arranged accompaniment
2005 Orchestra or other ensemble
Piano or organ
2006 Collections
2007 Separate works
Services
Class here cyclical choral works composed to liturgical or nonliturgical texts whether or not for use within the church or other sacred service
For individual parts of a liturgical (e.g. Credo) or nonliturgical service set as separate compositions, see M2020+
Roman Catholic
Masses
Settings of the Ordinary. Requiems
Complete works
2010 Accompaniment of orchestra or other ensemble
2011 Vocal and chorus scores without accompaniment. Unaccompanied works
2013 Accompaniment of organ, piano, or other instrument
Including vocal scores with organ or piano accompaniment of works with original accompaniment of orchestra, etc.
2013.5 Unison voices
2014 Excerpts
2014.5 Settings of Propers
Class here settings with or without the Ordinary
For requiems, see M2010+
2014.6 Offices and other services
2015 Orthodox
Anglican
2016 Collections
Separate works
2016.2 Morning and Evening service
Including works with or without Communion service
2016.3 Morning service

Vocal music
Sacred vocal music
Services
Anglican
Separate works -- Continued
2016.4 Evening service
For sets of vesper prayers, hymns, etc., see M2079.x96, M2099.x96, and M2114.x96
2016.5 Communion service
2016.6 Chant settings
Including services with or without accompaniment
2016.7 Unaccompanied services
2016.8 Special services
Including Office of the Dead, Burial service, Benediction service, etc.
2017 Lutheran
2017.2 Other Protestant
2017.6 Jewish
Class here services with originally composed music and collections of such services, except those for cantor without accompaniment
For services for cantor without accompaniment and collections containing both traditional and originally composed music, see M2186+
Duets, trios, etc. for solo voices
Accompaniment of orchestra or other ensemble, or electronic accompaniment
2018 Full scores
2019 Vocal scores with piano or organ accompaniment
Accompaniment of keyboard or other instrument, or unaccompanied
Class here works whose performance by solo voices is specifically indicated
For part-songs, motets, etc., that may be performed by either solo voices or chorus, see M2060+
Duets
2019.2 Collections
2019.3 Separate works
Trios, quartets, etc.
2019.4 Collections
2019.5 Separate works
Choruses
Choruses with orchestra, other ensemble, or electronic accompaniment
Class here choruses, cantatas, etc., with or without solo voices
Cf. M2000+, Oratorios
Cf. M2010+, Services
Mixed voices
Full scores

Vocal music
Sacred vocal music
Choruses
Choruses with orchestra, other ensemble, or electronic accompaniment
Mixed voices
Full scores -- Continued
Orchestral accompaniment
2020 General
2020.3 With recitation
2021 Other accompaniment
Class here works with accompaniment of string orchestra, band, other ensemble of two or more instruments, or electronic accompaniment
2022 Vocal and chorus scores without accompaniment
Vocal and chorus scores with piano or organ accompaniment
2023 General
2023.3 With recitation
Excerpts
2025 Original accompaniment
Arranged accompaniment
2026 Orchestra, etc.
Piano or organ
2027 Collections
2028 Separate works
Men's voices
2029 Full scores
2029.5 Vocal and chorus scores without accompaniment
2030 Vocal scores with piano or organ accompaniment
Excerpts
2031 Orchestral, etc., accompaniment
2032 Piano or organ accompaniment
Treble voices
2033 Full scores
2033.5 Vocal and chorus scores without accompaniment
2034 Vocal scores with piano or organ accompaniment
Excerpts
2035 Orchestral, etc., accompaniment
2036 Piano or organ accompaniment
Unison voices, see M2101.5

Vocal music
Sacred vocal music
Choruses -- Continued
Choruses, part-songs, etc., with accompaniment of keyboard or other solo instrument, or unaccompanied
Class here choruses, with or without solo voices, and part-songs, anthems, motets, etc., that may be performed by either chorus or solo voices
Class works in the following priority unless otherwise noted: 1) by type of accompaniment or unaccompanied; 2) by special text; 3) by special season or occasion; and 4) by type of chorus
For works whose performance by solo voices is specifically indicated, see M2019.2+

2060 Collections of accompanied and unaccompanied works
Accompaniment of keyboard instrument
Collections
Including collections that contain some works with accompaniment of other solo instrument
2061 Two or more types of chorus
2062 Mixed voices
2063 Men's voices
2064 Treble voices
Special seasons and occasions
2065 Christmas
2066 Easter
2067 Thanksgiving. Harvest
2068.A-Z Other, A-Z
2068.A4 Advent
2068.A5 All Saints Day
2068.A6 Ascension Day
2068.C2 Candlemas
2068.C75 Corpus Christi Festival
2068.E5 Epiphany
2068.F3 Father's Day
2068.G5 Good Friday
2068.H56 Holy Saturday
Holy Thursday, see M2068.M35
2068.H58 Holy Week
2068.H6 Holy Year
2068.L5 Lent. Passiontide
2068.M33 Marian feasts
2068.M35 Maundy Thursday
2068.M6 Mother's Day
2068.N5 New Year
2068.P4 Palm Sunday
Passiontide, see M2068.L5
Pentecost Festival, see M2068.W4

Vocal music
Sacred vocal music
Choruses
Choruses, part-songs, etc.,
with accompaniment of keyboard
or other solo instrument, or unaccompanied
Accompaniment of keyboard instrument
Collections
Special seasons and occasions
Other, A-Z -- Continued

2068.R3 Reformation Day
2068.T5 Trinity Sunday
2068.W4 Whitsuntide. Pentecost Festival
By religion or denomination
2069 Catholic
Orthodox, see M2080
Protestant, see M2060+
Jewish, see M2079.5
Separate works
2072 Mixed voices
2073 Men's voices
2074 Treble voices
Special seasons and occasions
2075 Christmas
2076 Easter
2077 Thanksgiving. Harvest
2078.A-Z Other, A-Z
2078.A4 Advent
2078.A5 All Saints Day
2078.A6 Ascension Day
2078.C2 Candlemas
2078.C75 Corpus Christi Festival
2078.E5 Epiphany
2078.F3 Father's Day
2078.G5 Good Friday
2078.H56 Holy Saturday
Holy Thursday, see M2078.M35
2078.H58 Holy Week
2078.H6 Holy Year
2078.L5 Lent. Passiontide
2078.M33 Marian feasts
2078.M35 Maundy Thursday
2078.M6 Mother's Day
2078.N5 New Year
2078.P4 Palm Sunday
Passiontide, see M2078.L5
Pentecost Festival, see M2078.W4
2078.R3 Reformation Day
2078.T5 Trinity Sunday
2078.W4 Whitsuntide. Pentecost Festival

Vocal music
Sacred vocal music
Choruses
Choruses, part-songs, etc.,
with accompaniment of keyboard
or other solo instrument, or unaccompanied
Accompaniment of keyboard instrument
Separate works -- Continued
2079.A-Z Special texts. By language, A-Z
(Table M6)
Including special parts of a liturgical
text set as separate compositions
For special texts not listed in Table M6
see the medium of performance, e.g.,
M2072, for Domine probasti me (Psalm
139) for mixed chorus with keyboard
accompaniment
By religion or denomination
2079.5 Jewish
Class here collections and separate works
2080 Orthodox
Class here collections and separate works
Accompaniment of instrument other than keyboard
instrument
For works for special seasons and occasions,
see M2065+
For works with special texts, see M2079.A+
2080.4 Two or more types of chorus
Class here collections only
2080.5 Mixed voices
2080.6 Men's voices
2080.7 Treble voices
Unaccompanied
Collections
2081 Two or more types of chorus
2082 Mixed voices
2083 Men's voices
2084 Treble voices
Special seasons and occasions
2085 Christmas
2086 Easter
2087 Thanksgiving. Harvest
2088.A-Z Other, A-Z
2088.A4 Advent
2088.A5 All Saints Day
2088.A6 Ascension Day
2088.C2 Candlemas
2088.C75 Corpus Christi Festival
2088.E5 Epiphany
2088.F3 Father's Day
2088.G5 Good Friday
2088.H56 Holy Saturday
Holy Thursday, see M2088.M35

Vocal music
Sacred vocal music
Choruses
Choruses, part-songs, etc., with accompaniment of keyboard or other solo instrument, or unaccompanied
Unaccompanied
Collections
Special seasons and occasions
Other, A-Z -- Continued

2088.H58 Holy Week
2088.H6 Holy Year
2088.L5 Lent. Passiontide
2088.M33 Marian feasts
2088.M35 Maundy Thursday
2088.M6 Mother's Day
2088.N5 New Year
2088.P4 Palm Sunday
Passiontide, see M2088.L5
Pentecost Festival, see M2088.W4
2088.R3 Reformation Day
2088.T5 Trinity Sunday
2088.W4 Whitsuntide. Pentecost Festival
By religion or denomination
2089 Catholic
2090 Protestant
Islamic, see M2099.3
Jewish, see M2099.5
Orthodox, see M2100
Separate works
2092 Mixed voices
2093 Men's voices
2094 Treble voices
Special seasons and occasions
2095 Christmas
2096 Easter
2097 Thanksgiving. Harvest
2098.A-Z Other, A-Z
2098.A4 Advent
2098.A5 All Saints Day
2098.A6 Ascension Day
2098.C2 Candlemas
2098.C75 Corpus Christi Festival
2098.E5 Epiphany
2098.F3 Father's Day
2098.G5 Good Friday
2098.H56 Holy Saturday
Holy Thursday, see M2098.M35
2098.H58 Holy Week
2098.H6 Holy Year
2098.L5 Lent. Passiontide
2098.M33 Marian feasts
2098.M35 Maundy Thursday

Vocal music
Sacred vocal music
Choruses
Choruses, part-songs, etc.,
with accompaniment of keyboard
or other solo instrument, or unaccompanied
Unaccompanied
Separate works
Special seasons and occasions
Other, A-Z -- Continued

2098.M6 Mother's Day
2098.N5 New Year
2098.P4 Palm Sunday
Passiontide, see M2098.L5
Pentecost Festival, see M2098.W4
2098.R3 Reformation Day
2098.T5 Trinity Sunday
2098.W4 Whitsuntide. Pentecost Festival
2099.A-Z Special texts. By language, A-Z
(Table M6)
Including special parts of a liturgical
text set as separate compositions
For special texts not listed in Table M6
see the medium of performance, e.g.,
M2092, for Domine probasti me (Psalm
139) for unaccompanied chorus
By religion or denomination
2099.3 Islamic
Class here collections and separate works
2099.5 Jewish
Class here collections and separate works
Orthodox
2100 Collections
2100.2 Separate works
2101 Choruses, etc., in tonic sol-fa notation
2101.5 Unison choruses
Cf. M2013.5, Masses for unison chorus
Songs
Including arias, solo cantatas, etc., with or
without obligato chorus or refrain
Orchestral, etc., accompaniment
Original compositions
2102 Collections
Including collections of both original and
arranged compositions
Separate songs
Full scores
2103 Orchestral accompaniment

Vocal music
Sacred vocal music
Songs
Orchestral, etc., accompaniment
Original compositions
Separate songs
Full scores -- Continued

2103.3 Other accompaniment
Class here works with accompaniment of string orchestra, band, other ensemble of two or more instruments, or electronic accompaniment
For accompaniment of piano and one other instrument, see M2113.3

2104 Vocal scores with piano or organ accompaniment

Arrangements
Collections

2105 Full scores

2106 Vocal scores with piano or organ accompaniment

Separate songs

2107 Full scores

2108 Vocal scores with piano or organ accompaniment

Accompaniment of piano, etc., and unaccompanied
Including accompaniment of one instrument of any type and of two instruments, one of which is chordal
Collections
For Jewish liturgy and ritual, see M2186+

2110 Two or more composers

2112 One composer

Separate songs

2113 Accompaniment of one instrument

2113.2 Unaccompanied

2113.3 Accompaniment of piano, etc., and one other instrument

2113.4 Song cycles

2114.A-Z Special texts. By language, A-Z (Table M6)
Including individual parts of liturgical texts set as separate compositions
For special texts not listed in Table M6 see the medium of performance, e.g., M2113, for Domine probasti me (Psalm 139) for solo voice with keyboard accompaniment

By religion or denomination

2114.1.A-Z Protestant. By denomination, A-Z

2114.2 Orthodox

2114.3 Jewish
Cf. M2187, special holidays, rites, and portions of the liturgy

Vocal music
Sacred vocal music
Songs
Accompaniment of piano, etc., and unaccompanied
Separate songs
By religion or denomination -- Continued
2114.4.A-Z Other religions or denominations, A-Z
Special seasons and occasions
2114.5 Christmas
2114.6 Easter
2114.7 Thanksgiving. Harvest
Other, A-Z
2114.8.A4 Advent
2114.8.A5 All Saints Day
2114.8.A6 Ascension Day
2114.8.C2 Candlemas
2114.8.C75 Corpus Christi Festival
2114.8.E5 Epiphany
2114.8.F3 Father's Day
2114.8.G5 Good Friday
2114.8.H56 Holy Saturday
Holy Thursday, see M2114.8.M35
2114.8.H58 Holy Week
2114.8.H6 Holy Year
2114.8.L5 Lent. Passiontide
2114.8.M33 Marian feasts
2114.8.M35 Maundy Thursday
2114.8.M6 Mother's Day
2114.8.N5 New Year
2114.8.P4 Palm Sunday
Passiontide, see M2114.8.L5
Pentecost Festival, see M2114.8.W4
2114.8.R3 Reformation Day
2114.8.T5 Trinity Sunday
2114.8.W4 Whitsuntide. Pentecost Festival
Hymnals. Hymn collections
For hymnals with words only, including those with tunes indicated, see BV1+
2115 General
Including collections of hymns of Christian and other religions
2115.5 Descant collections, with or without their hymns
Christian
United States
2116 Through 1820
1821-

Vocal music
Sacred vocal music
Hymnals. Hymn collections
Christian
United States
1821- -- Continued

2117 General
Class here multi-denominational and non-denominational hymnals in English or mainly in English
For multi-denominational and non-denominational hymnals entirely or mainly in languages other than English, see M2132.A+

By denomination
Including hymnals in languages other than English

2119 Catholic
2120 Orthodox
Protestant
General, see M2117
2122 Baptist
2123 Congregational
Cf. M2131.U62, United Church of Christ
2124.A-Z Dutch and other Reformed
Cf. M2131.U62, United Church of Christ
2124.C55 Christian Reformed Church
2124.D7 Dutch Reformed (Reformed Church in the United States)
2124.G3 German Reformed (Reformed Church in the United States)
2125 Episcopal
2126 Lutheran
2127 Methodist
2128 Moravian
2129 Mormon
2130 Presbyterian
2131.A-Z Other, A-Z
2131.A15 Aaronic Order
2131.A3 Adventist
Cf. M2131.S3, Seventh-Day Adventist
2131.A4 Amish
2131.A45 Anabaptist
2131.A5 Apostolic Christian Church
Avesta, see M2131.M2
2131.B6 Brethren in Christ Church
2131.C33 Církev Československá
2131.C43 Christian Catholic Apostolic Church in Zion. Dowieites

Vocal music
Sacred vocal music
Hymnals. Hymn collections
Christian
United States
1821-
By denomination
Protestant
Other, A-Z -- Continued

2131.C5 Christian Science. Church of Christ, Scientist
2131.C53 Christ's Church of the Golden Rule
2131.C54 Church of Christ (Holiness) U.S.A.
2131.C55 Church of Divine Man
2131.C57 Church of God (Anderson, Ind.)
2131.C6 Church of God, Holiness
2131.C63 Church of God General Conference
2131.C64 Church of God, the Eternal
2131.C65 Church of the Brethren
2131.C68 Church of the Nazarene
2131.D4 Disciples of Christ
2131.D5 Divine Science Church (U.S.)
Dowieites, see M2131.C43
Ephrata Cloister, see M2116
2131.E8 Evangelical Mission Covenant Church of America
2131.F8 Free Methodist
Cf. M2127, Methodist
2131.F9 Society of Friends (Quakers)
Holiness (Church of Christ), see M2131.C54
Holiness (Church of God), see M2131.C6
2131.H87 Hutterian Brethren
2131.I2 I AM religious activity
2131.I55 International Churches of Christ
2131.I57 Intervarsity Christian Fellowship of the United States of America
2131.J49 Jews for Jesus
2131.M2 Mazdaznan. Avesta
2131.M4 Mennonite Church
2131.M6 Monism
2131.M7 Moral Re-armament
New Jerusalem Church, see M2131.S8
2131.P4 Pentecostal Holiness
2131.P5 Pillar of Fire
Quakers, see M2131.F9
2131.R3 International Association of Religious Science Churches
2131.S3 Seventh-Day Adventist
Cf. M2131.A3, Adventist
2131.S4 Shakers
2131.S44 Church of the Social Revolution
2131.S5 Spiritualist

Vocal music
Sacred vocal music
Hymnals. Hymn collections
Christian
United States
1821-
By denomination
Protestant
Other, A-Z -- Continued
2131.S8 Swedenborgian (New Jerusalem Church)
2131.T78 True Jesus Church, U.S.A.
2131.U5 Unitarian churches. Unitarian Universalist Association
Cf. M2131.U7, Universalist Church
2131.U6 United Brethren in Christ
2131.U62 United Church of Christ
Cf. M2123, Congregational
Cf. M2124.A+, Dutch and other Reformed
2131.U63 United Church of Religious Science
2131.U65 Unity School of Christianity
2131.U7 Universalist Church
Cf. M2131.U5, Unitarian churches and Unitarian Universalist Association
2131.W67 Worldwide Church of God
2132.A-Z Multi- and non-denominational hymnals. By language, A-Z
For Latin hymnals published in the United States, see M2119
For multi-denominational and non-denominational hymnals entirely or mainly in English, see M2117
2132.C6 Croatian
2132.S3 Slovak
2132.T2 Tagalog
2133 Other North American countries (not A-Z)
2134.A-Z Central and South America. By language, A-Z
Europe. By language, A-Z
2135 Dutch
2136 English
2137 French
2138 German
2139 Russian
2140.A-Z Scandinavian languages
2140.D3 Danish
2140.N6 Norwegian
2140.S8 Swedish
2142.A-Z Other, A-Z
2142.A42 Albanian
2142.A6 Armenian
2142.B38 Basque

Vocal music
Sacred vocal music
Hymnals. Hymn collections
Christian
Europe. By language, A-Z
Other, A-Z -- Continued

2142.B8 Bulgarian
Croatian, see M2142.S35
2142.C9 Czech
2142.F4 Finnish
2142.F7 Frisian
2142.G3 Galician
2142.G7 Greek
2142.H9 Hungarian
2142.I2 Icelandic
2142.I5 Irish
2142.I6 Italian
(2142.L17) Lapp
See M2142.S26
2142.L2 Latin
2142.L23 Latvian
2142.L5 Lithuanian
2142.P5 Polish
2142.R6 Romanian
2142.S26 Sami
2142.S35 Serbo-Croatian
2142.S4 Slovak
2142.S47 Sorbian
2142.S5 Spanish
2142.S7 Sami
2142.U7 Ukrainian
2142.W3 Welsh
2143 Other regions and countries (not A-Z)
2144 Jewish
2145.A-Z Other religions, A-Z
e.g.
2145.B34 Bahai
Including National Spiritual Assembly of the Bahá'ís of the United States
2145.B8 Buddhism
2145.H55 Hinduism
2145.S57 Sikhism
2146 Separate hymns

Vocal music
Sacred vocal music -- Continued
Liturgy and ritual
Class here officially prescribed service music
Arrange chronologically unless otherwise stated
For other church music composed to sacred texts for use in church services, class as provided in the schedule, e.g., M2016, a Protestant Episcopal choral service by one or more composers; M2020, a Te Deum with orchestral accompaniment; M2079.L3, a Credo with organ accompaniment and Latin text; M2079.E3, with English text; M2099.E6, a Magnificat in English for men's and boys' voices unaccompanied (English text), M2115-M2146, hymnals, etc.; M2, historical publications
For manuscripts and publications mainly rubrical, with the music merely one of the liturgical functions, see BL1+
Roman Catholic Church
2147 Copyists' manuscripts and their facsimiles
Arrange by century in Roman numerals followed by M with accession number, e.g., M2147 XII M13
Printed music
For liturgical music of individual dioceses, see M2154.2.A+
For liturgical music of individual orders and congregations, see M2154.4.A+
For liturgical music of other western rites, see M2154.6.A+
2148.A-Z Graduals. By language, A-Z
Under each language:
.x *Complete work. By date*
.x2 *Selections. By date*
Propers
2148.2.A-Z Collections. By compiler or publisher, A-Z
Arrange by title if compiler or publisher is unknown
Under each compiler, etc.:
.x *Complete work. By date*
.x2 *Selections. By date*
2148.23.A-Z Praefationes particulares. By language, A-Z
Apply table at M2148.A-Z
2148.3.A-Z Separate works. By feast day or person to whom the mass was dedicated, A-Z, and date
Advent
2148.3.A31 First Sunday of Advent
2148.3.A32 Second Sunday of Advent
2148.3.A88 Assumption of the Blessed Virgin Mary
2148.3.B59 Blessed Virgin Mary, Saint

M

Vocal music
Sacred vocal music
Liturgy and ritual
Roman Catholic Church
Printed music
Graduals. By language, A-Z, and date
Propers
Separate works. By feast day, or person to whom the mass was dedicated, A-Z, and date -- Continued
Christmas

2148.3.C5 Christmas Eve
2148.3.C55 Christmas Day
Specific masses
2148.3.C551 1st Mass
2148.3.C552 2nd Mass
2148.3.C553 3rd Mass
2148.3.C6 Circumcision. Octave Day of Christmas
2148.3.C65 Mass, Common, of a confessor not a bishop
2148.3.C67 Corpus Christi Festival
2148.3.D4 Mass on the day of death or burial
2148.3.E2 Easter Sunday
2148.3.E6 Epiphany
Sundays after Epiphany
2148.3.E61 1st Sunday
2148.3.E62 2nd Sunday
2148.3.E63 3rd Sunday
2148.3.H64 Holy Thursday
2148.3.I46 Immaculate Heart of Mary
2148.3.J35 James, the Greater, Saint
2148.3.J4 Joan, of Arc, Saint
2148.3.M3 Feasts of the Blessed Virgin Mary throughout the year
For individual feasts, see .A88, .B59, etc.
Octave Day of Christmas, see M2148.3.C6
2148.3.P3 Passion Sunday
2148.3.P45 Pentecost Festival
Sundays after Pentecost Festival
2148.3.P4501 1st Sunday
2148.3.P4502 2nd Sunday
2148.3.P4503 3rd Sunday
2148.3.P4516 16th Sunday
2148.3.P66 Mass, Common, of one or more Popes
2148.3.T48 Teresa, of Avila, Saint
Ordinaries
2148.4.A-Z Kyriales. Collections of ordinaries. By language, A-Z
Apply table at M2148.A-Z
2148.5.A-Z Single ordinaries

Vocal music
Sacred vocal music
Liturgy and ritual
Roman Catholic Church
Printed music
Gradicals

	Vocal music
	Sacred vocal music
	Liturgy and ritual
	Roman Catholic Church
	Printed music
	Graduals
	Kyriales. By language, A-Z, and date
	Single ordinaries -- Continued
2148.5.A11-A28	Numbered masses. By number, 1-18, and date
2148.5.A5-Z	Masses for special events. By event, A-Z, and date
2149.A-Z	Antiphonaries. By language, A-Z Apply table at M2148.A-Z
2149.2.A-Z	Special sections, A-Z Subarrange by language and add date
2149.2.B5	Benedictions
2149.2.C6	Compline
2149.2.H9	Hymnary
2149.2.L35	Lauds
2149.2.L4	Lectionary
2149.2.M4	Matins
2149.2.O2	O antiphons
2149.2.P8	Psalters and collections of psalms
2149.2.V4	Vesperals and collections of vespers
2149.3.A-Z	Collections of offices. By compiler or publisher, A-Z Subarrange by title if compiler or publisher is unknown Apply table at M2148.2.A-Z
2149.4.A-Z	Holy Week rite
2149.4.A1A-Z	Collections. By language, A-Z Apply table at M2148.A-Z
2149.4.A5-Z	Individual services. By service, A-Z Subarrange by language Apply table at M2148.A-Z
2149.4.C35	Cantus Passionis
2149.4.C353	Cantus Passionis. Passio Secundum Joannem
2149.4.C356	Cantus Passionis. Passio Secundum Matthaeum
2149.4.E25	Easter preconium
2149.4.G7	Good Friday
2149.4.H68	Holy Saturday
2149.4.H69	Holy Thursday
2149.4.P34	Palm Sunday
2149.42.A-Z	Holy Week offices. By language, A-Z Apply table at M2148.A-Z
2149.5.A-Z	Single offices, A-Z Subarrange by date
2149.5.A6	Anthony of Egypt, Saint
	Christmas
2149.5.C5	General

Vocal music
Sacred vocal music
Liturgy and ritual
Roman Catholic church
Printed music
Antiphonaries. By language, A-Z
Single offices, A-Z
Christmas -- Continued
Vespers, see M2149.5.V525
Office for the dead

2149.5.D4 General
2149.5.D44 Matins
2149.5.D48 Vespers
2149.5.D56 Dionysius, the Areopagite, Saint
2149.5.L52 Little office of the Blessed Virgin Mary
2149.5.N5 Nikolaus, von der Flüe, Saint
2149.5.V5-V58 Vespers
2149.5.V5 General
2149.5.V52 Ascension
2149.5.V525 Christmas. 2d Vespers
2149.5.V53 Corpus Christi Festival
2149.5.V54 Easter
2149.5.V545 Saint Joseph
2149.5.V55 Marian feasts
2149.5.V56 Pentecost Festival
2149.5.V57 Solemnity of the Most Holy Rosary
2149.5.V575 Sunday
2149.5.V58 Trinity
2149.6 Processionals
Subarrange by date
Special ceremonies and occasions
2150 General
2150.2.A-Z Collections of chants. By compiler or publisher, A-Z
Apply table at M2148.2.A-Z
2150.3.A-Z Particular ceremonies, A-Z
Under each ceremony:
.x *Complete work. By date*
.x2 *Selections. By date*
2150.3.B46-B462 Benediction of the Blessed Sacrament
2150.3.B6-B62 Blessing of a church organ
2150.3.B87-B872 Burial rite
2150.3.C58-C582 Confirmation
Consecration of a church, see M2150.3.D42+
2150.3.D42-D422 Dedication of a church
2150.3.F57-F572 First communion
2150.3.F67-F672 Forty hours of adoration
2150.4.A-Z Particular occasions, A-Z
Under each occasion:
.x *Complete work. By date*
.x2 *Selections. By date*
2150.4.C35-C352 Candlemas
2150.4.C5-C52 Christmas

Vocal music
Sacred vocal music
Liturgy and ritual
Roman Catholic Church
Printed music -- Continued

2151.A-Z Liber usualis. By language, A-Z
Apply table at M2148.A-Z
2152 Directories and manuals for choirs
Miscellaneous collections of liturgical music for general use
2153 General
2153.2.A-Z Collections of chants. By compiler or title, A-Z
Special Roman liturgies and rituals
2154.2.A-Z Diocesan, A-Z
e.g.
2154.2.C64 Cologne
2154.2.L4 Leavenworth
2154.2.L9 Luxemburg
2154.2.M4 Meissen
2154.2.M83 Münster
2154.2.P6 Pittsburgh
2154.2.Q4 Quebec
2154.2.S34 Salzburg
2154.2.S4 Sées
2154.4.A-Z Orders and congregations, A-Z
2154.4.A9 Augustinian
2154.4.B45 Benedictine
2154.4.C34 Camaldolite
2154.4.C36 Capuchin
2154.4.C37 Carmelite
2154.4.C6 Cistercian
2154.4.D63 Discalced Trinitarian
2154.4.D65 Dominican
2154.4.F7 Franciscan
2154.4.H5 Hieronymite
2154.4.M5 Mercedarian
2154.4.P4 Passionist
2154.4.P74 Premonstratensian
2154.4.S58 Sisters of Charity of Saint Vincent de Paul
2154.4.S6 Sisters of the Good Shepherd
2154.4.U8 Ursuline
2154.6.A-Z Non-Roman liturgies and rituals, A-Z
Subarrange by uniform title and add date
2154.6.A45 Ambrosian
2154.6.A76 Armenian
2154.6.M7 Mozarabic
Modern schisms from the Roman Catholic Church
2155.5 Old Catholic Church
2155.6 Polish Catholic Church
Orthodox churches

Vocal music
Sacred vocal music
Liturgy and ritual
Orthodox Churches -- Continued
2156 Copyists' manuscripts and their facsimiles
Arrange by century in Roman numerals followed by M with accession number, e.g., M2156 XIII M1
Printed music. By denomination, ethnic group, or language
2157 Greek
2158 Russian
2159.1 Bulgarian
2159.2 Czechoslovak
2159.3 Serbian
2159.5 Romanian
2160.2 Armenian
2160.3 Chaldean (i.e. Nestorian)
2160.4 Coptic
2160.5 Ethiopic
2160.6 Georgian
2160.65 Syrian
2160.67.A-Z Other vernacular or ethnic groups, A-Z
e.g.
2160.67.E5 English
Orthodox churches in communion with Rome (Uniat)
2160.7 General
Byzantine rite
2160.71 General
2160.72 Bulgarian
2160.73 Greek
2160.74 Italo-Albanian
2160.75 Melkite
2160.76 Romanian
2160.77 Russian
2160.78 Ukrainian
Other Eastern rites
2160.8 General
Armenian, see M2154.6.A76
2160.82 Chaldean
2160.83 Coptic
2160.84 Ethiopic
2160.85 Malabaric
2160.86 Maronite
2160.87 Syrian
Protestant churches
Class here manuscripts and printed music
2161 General
2162 Baptist
2163 Congregational
2164 Dutch and other Reformed
Anglican Communion

Vocal music
Sacred vocal music
Liturgy and ritual
Protestant Churches
Anglican Communion -- Continued
Church of England
2167 Book of Common Prayer
Including its immediate precursors
2168.2 Morning service
2168.3 Evening service
2168.4 Order of the Communion
2168.5 Other offices
2168.6 Chants
Class here miscellaneous and special collections
2168.7 Directories, manuals, handbooks, etc.
2168.9 Other
Protestant Episcopal Church in the U.S.A.
2169 Book of Common Prayer
Including its immediate precursors
2170.2 Morning service
2170.3 Evening service
2170.4 Order of the Communion
2170.5 Other offices
2170.6 Chants
Class here miscellaneous and special collections
2170.7 Directories, manuals, handbooks, etc.
2170.9 Other
2171.A-Z Other. By country, A-Z
e.g.
2171.C3 Anglican Church of Canada
Lutheran
2172 European publications
2173 American publications
2175 Methodist
2177 Moravian
2179 Mormon
2181 Presbyterian
2183.A-Z Other denominations, A-Z
2184.A-Z Other Christian churches, A-Z
Jewish
Class here traditional music intended for use in the synagogue
Including services with originally composed music for cantor without accompaniment and collections containing both traditional and originally composed music
Cf. M2017.6, Jewish services
2186 General
2187 Special holidays, rites, and portions of the liturgy
2188.A-Z Other non-Christian religions, A-Z

Vocal music
Sacred vocal music
Liturgy and ritual
Other non-Christian religions, A-Z -- Continued
2188.B8 Buddhism
2188.H5 Hinduism
2188.S5 Shinto
2188.S8 Sufism
Sacred vocal music for children
Dramatic and choral works
Class here oratorios, masses, cantatas, anthems, Sunday School services, pageants, etc.
2190 General
2191.A-Z Special seasons and occasions, A-Z
2191.A4 Advent
2191.C4 Children's Day
2191.C5 Christmas
2191.E2 Easter
2191.E6 Epiphany
2191.F38 Father's Day
Harvest, see M2191.T5
2191.H6 Holy Week
2191.L5 Lent. Passiontide
2191.M6 Mother's Day
2191.P3 Palm Sunday
Passiontide, see M2191.L5
2191.R2 Rally Day
2191.T5 Thanksgiving. Harvest
Songs
Class here part-songs and solo songs
Collections
2193 General
Including Sunday or Bible School songbooks, etc.
By religion or denomination
2194 Roman Catholic
2194.3 Jewish
2196 Separate songs
Popular religious or devotional music
Class here gospel, revival, and temperence songs, contemporary Christian music, etc.
2198 Collections
2199 Separate songs
5000 Unidentified compositions
Including excerpts, fragments, etc., published or in manuscript

Literature on music
Periodicals. Serials
Class here general periodicals in the field of music
Class periodicals consisting entirely of music in subclass M
Class periodicals on specific topics with the topic, e.g., Contemporary Christian music in ML3187.5, orchestral program notes in MT125

1 United States
Foreign
4 Through 1800
5 1801-
Directories. Almanacs
12 International
United States
13 General works
14.A-Z By region or state, A-Z (Table M1)
15.A-Z By city, A-Z
17 Professions
18 Music trade
19 Other (not A-Z)
21.A-Z Other regions or countries, A-Z
Societies and organizations
25 General works
26.A-Z International. By society or organization, A-Z
Under each society or organization:
.x *General works*
.x3 *Constitution, by-laws, lists of members, etc. By date*
.x4 *History*
.x5 *Annual reports. By date*
.x6 *Special (irregular) reports*
.x7 *Programs. By date*
Cf. ML40-44, Opera, concert, etc., programs
.x9 *Other*
27.A-Z National. By country and society or organization, A-Z
Assign two Cutters, the first for the country, the second for the name of the society or organization
Extend the second Cutter as follows:
.x *General works*
.x3 *Constitution, by-laws, lists of members, etc. By date*
.x4 *History*
.x5 *Annual reports. By date*
.x6 *Special (irregular) reports*
.x7 *Programs. By date*
Cf. ML40-44, Opera, concert, etc., programs
.x9 *Other*

Societies and organizations -- Continued

28.A-Z Local. By city and society or organization, A-Z

Assign two Cutters, the first for the city, the second for the name of the society or organization

Apply table at ML27.A-Z

Special collections

Class here unique collections. The Library of Congress will use ML29-31 as shown

Endowed collections

29 Elizabeth Sprague Coolidge Foundation

30 Other

31 Other special collections

Institutions

For educational institutions, see MT4+

For works emphasizing the history of individual regions or countries, see ML198+

32.A-Z National. By country and institution, A-Z

Assign two Cutters, the first for the country, the second for the name of the institution

Apply table at ML27.A-Z

33.A-Z Local. By city and institution, A-Z

Assign two Cutters, the first for the city, the second for the name of the institution

Apply table at ML27.A-Z

Festivals. Congresses

Including performance festivals

For competitions, see ML75.5+

For congresses on specific topics, see the topic, e.g., Wind instruments, ML929.5

35 General works

36.A-Z International. By festival or congress, A-Z

Under each festival or congress:

.x General works

.x4 History

.x5 Annual reports. By date

.x6 Special (irregular) reports

.x7 Programs. By date

Cf. ML40-44, Opera, concert, etc., programs

.x9 Other

Festivals. Congresses -- Continued
37.A-Z National. By country and festival or congress, A-Z
Assign two Cutters, the first for the country, the second for the name of the festival or congress
Extend the second Cutter as follows:
.x General works
.x4 History
.x5 Annual reports. By date
.x6 Special (irregular) reports
.x7 Programs. By date
Cf., ML40-44, Opera, concert, etc., programs
.x9 Other
38.A-Z Local. By city and festival or congress, A-Z
Assign two Cutters, the first for the city, the second for the name of the festival or congress
Apply table at ML37.A-Z
Programs
Class here programs not classed in ML25-ML38
For programs containing extensive analytical notes, see MT90+
40.A-Z Operas
40.A1-A39 Collections. By compiler or title
40.A4-Z Individual programs. By city and institution, A-Z
Assign two Cutters, the first for the city, the second for the name of the institution
42.A-Z Concerts
42.A1-A39 Collections. By compiler or title
42.A4-Z Individual programs. By city and institution, A-Z
Assign two Cutters, the first for the city, the second for the name of the institution
44.A-Z Other
44.A1-A39 Collections. By compiler or title
44.A4-Z Individual programs. By city and institution, A-Z
Assign two Cutters, the first for the city, the second for the name of the institution
45 Circulars and advertisements
Class here miscellaneous circulars and advertisements not classed in ML25-ML38, or ML140-ML155
46 Scrapbooks
Librettos. Scenarios
For works about librettos, see ML2110
47 Miscellaneous collections
Operas
Including operettas, musicals, Singspiele, sacred operas, etc.
Collections
48 Two or more composers (or authors)
49 One composer (or author)
Separate works

Librettos. Scenarios
Operas
Separate works -- Continued
50 1800- (non-U.S. imprints), or 1850- (U.S. imprints). By composer
Subarrange by title
Use .Z99 for works by three or more composers, works for which the music is not originally composed but compiled from various sources, or works for which no composer is identified
50.2 To 1800 (non-U.S. imprints). By title
Subarrange by composer or author
50.6 To 1850 (U.S. imprints). By title
Subarrange by composer or author
50.7 Ballad operas. By title
50.9 Parodies
For parodies of Richard Wagner and his works, see ML410.W1A298A+
Ballets, masques, pantomimes, etc.
51 Collections
Separate works
52 1800- (non-U.S. imprints), or 1850- (U.S. imprints). By composer
Subarrange by title
Use .Z99 for works by three or more composers, works for which the music is not originally composed but compiled from various sources, or works for which no composer is identified
52.2 To 1800 (non-U.S. imprints). By title
Subarrange by composer or author
52.6 To 1850 (U.S. imprints). By title
Subarrange by composer or author
Film operas
52.65 Collections
52.7 Separate works. By composer
Subarrange by title
Use .Z99 for works by three or more composers, works for which the music is not originally composed but compiled from various sources, or works for which no composer is identified
Radio operas
52.75 Collections
52.8 Separate works. By composer
Subarrange by title
Use .Z99 for works by three or more composers, works for which the music is not originally composed but compiled from various sources, or works for which no composer is identified
Oratorios
52.85 Collections
Separate works

Librettos. Scenarios
Oratorios
Separate works -- Continued
53 1800- (non-U.S. imprints), or 1850- (U.S. imprints). By composer
Subarrange by title
Use .Z99 for works by three or more composers, works for which the music is not originally composed but compiled from various sources, or works for which no composer is identified
53.2 To 1800 (non-U.S. imprints). By title
Subarrange by composer or author
53.6 To 1850 (U.S. imprints). By title
Subarrange by composer or author
Cantatas, choruses, etc.
53.8 Collections
Separate works
54 1800- . By composer
Subarrange by title
Use .Z99 for works by three or more composers, works for which the music is not originally composed but compiled from various sources, or works for which no composer is identified
54.2 To 1800. By title
Subarrange by composer or author
Songs and cantatas for one voice, etc.
Including lyrics of popular songs
For collections of folk-song texts published without the music but intended for use in singing, e.g., songsters, see M1627+
For collections of folk-song texts published as poetry, see class P
54.6 1800-
54.7 To 1800
54.8 Other
Collected works (nonserial)
Addresses. Essays. Lectures
55 Several authors
Including Festschriften with contributions on various topics, by honoree
Class Festschriften with contributions on specific topics with the topic
60 Individual authors
e.g.
60.L24 Lanier, Sidney, 1842-1881
Special aspects of the subject as a whole
62 Governmental, municipal, etc., subvention of music
63 Topics not elsewhere provided for
Poems and other belles lettres about music
See class P
65 Anecdotes, humor, etc.
Cf. PN6231.M85, Wit and humor

Special aspects of the subject as a whole -- Continued
Quotations, maxims, etc., and birthday books
See subclass PN
67 Music in the home
68 Radio, television, etc., and music
Cf. ML3849, Philosophical works on the relations between music and other arts
Cf. PN1992.8.M87, Music videos
Law
See class K
Music as a profession
Including vocational guidance
Cf. ML3795, Musical life
70 General works
71 Registration of musicians, examination by government boards, standardization, etc.
Design of concert halls, opera houses, etc , see NA6820+
Construction of concert halls, opera houses, etc , see TH4711
Computers and music
Class here general works on the use of computers in the field of music
For works on computer music, see ML1379+
For works on computer sound processing, see MT723
For works on the computer as a musical instrument, see ML1093
For works on the techniques of composing computer music, see MT56
73 Periodicals. Societies. Serials
73.5 Congresses
74 General works
Computer software
For software catalogs, see ML158.8
74.3 General works
74.4.A-Z Individual programs and systems, A-Z
74.7 Computer network resources
Prizes, competitions, etc.
75.5 General works
76.A-Z Individual prizes, competitions, etc., A-Z
76.G7 Grammy Awards
Literary authors and music
Cf. ML3849, Philosophical works on the relations between music and other arts
79 Two or more authors
80.A-Z Individual authors, A-Z
e.g.
80.C25 Camões, Luiz de, 1524?-1580
80.S5 Shakespeare, William, 1564-1616
81 Musical prodigies
82 Women and music
83 Children and music

Special aspects of the subject as a whole -- Continued
85 Music in art. Musical instruments in art
Cf. ML3849, Philosophical works on the relations between music and other arts
86 Music on coins. Music on ceramics
For music on postage stamps and postmarks, see HE6183.M85
Portraits, caricatures, houses, etc., and iconography of musicians
Collections, two or more musicians
87.A1-A39 Of miscellaneous single items
87.A4-Z In book form
88.A-Z Individual musicians, A-Z
For Richard Wagner, see ML410.W196
89 Pictorial works
For illustrated title pages, see ML112.5
For pictorial works about special topics, see the topic, e.g., Jazz, see ML3505.8-ML3509
90 Writings of musicians (Collections)
For individual musicians, etc., see ML410+
Manuscripts, autographs, etc. Paleography
Cf. ML135, Bibliographies of manuscripts
93 General works
Miscellaneous collections of autographs, etc.
94 Manuscripts
94.5 Facsimiles
Literature, letters, etc. of individual musicians after 1600
For pre-1600 literature, see ML171
95 Manuscripts
95.5 Facsimiles
Compositions and musical sketches
For all manuscripts and facsimiles of liturgical music for the Catholic Church, see M2147
For all manuscripts and facsimiles of liturgical music for the Orthodox churches, see M2156
For historical collections, including facsimiles, of autograph and copyists' manuscripts, see M2+
For copyists' manuscripts intended as performing editions, see subclass M
96 Manuscripts
Class here autograph manuscripts of separate works and sketches by one composer, and collections of works and sketches by one or more composers
Facsimiles
Including sketches, with or without transcription, and sketches in transcription
For facsimiles of composers' autograph manuscripts intended as performing editions, see subclass M
96.4 Collections
Class here collections of works and sketches by one or more composers

Manuscripts, autographs, etc. Paleography
Compositions and musical sketches
Facsimiles -- Continued
96.5 Separate works
Dictionaries. Encyclopedias
100 General works
101.A-Z By region or country, A-Z
102.A-Z By topic, A-Z
102.A2 Accordion
102.B35 Bands
102.B5 Big bands
Including jazz bands
102.B6 Blues
102.B7 Brass instruments
102.C3 Carols
102.C45 Chants (plain, Gregorian, etc.)
Choral music, see ML102.V6
102.C5 Church music
102.C6 Computer music. Computers and music
102.C7 Country music
Dance bands, see ML102.B5
102.D85 Dulcimer
102.E4 Electronic music
102.F55 Flamenco
102.F66 Folk music
102.G2 Gagaku
102.G6 Gospel music
102.G8 Guitar
102.H56 Hindustani music
102.H95 Hymns
102.I5 Instruments (General)
102.J3 Jazz
Jazz bands, see ML102.B5
102.J4 Jewish music and musicians
102.K37 Karnatic music
102.K5 Keyboard instruments
102.M68 Motion picture music
102.M85 Music trade
Musical revues, comedies, etc., see ML102.M88
102.M88 Musicals. Revues
102.N49 New Age music
102.O6 Opera
102.O66 Orchestra
102.O7 Organ
102.P4 Percussion instruments
102.P5 Piano
102.P66 Popular music
102.R2 Raga
Revues, see ML102.M88
102.R4 Rhythm
102.R6 Rock music
102.S6 Songs
102.S65 Soul music

ML

Dictionaries. Encyclopedias
By topic, A-Z -- Continued
102.S67 Sound recordings
102.T3 Tala
102.T35 Tangos
102.T58 Titles of musical works
102.V4 Violin
102.V45 Violin and keyboard instrument
102.V6 Vocal music
Bio-bibliographical
For works on specific topics, see ML102.A+
105 International
106.A-Z National. By country, A-Z
United States
106.U3 General works
106.U4A-Z By region or state, A-Z (Table M1)
107.A-Z Local, A-Z
For regions or states of the United States, see ML106.U4A+
108 Terminological
109 Pronouncing
Music librarianship
Including cataloging, classification, etc.
For cataloging of sound recordings in general, see Z695.715
110 Periodicals. Societies. Serials
111 General works
111.5 Sound recording libraries and collecting
Music printing and publishing
112 General works
112.5 Music title pages
Including illustrated title pages
Bibliography
Class here bibliographies of music and bibliographies of works about music
112.8 Theory, practice, history
International
113 General works
By period
114 Through 1600
115 1601-1700
116 1701-1800
117 1801-1900
118 1901-
120.A-Z By region or country, A-Z
125.A-Z Local, A-Z
128.A-Z By topic, A-Z
128.A3 Accordion
Afro-American music, see ML128.B45
Afro-American spirituals, see ML128.S4
128.A45 Alleluia
Analysis, see ML128.A7
128.A67 Appalachian dulcimer

Bibliography
By topic, A-Z -- Continued

128.A7 Appreciation. Analysis
128.B17 Bagpipe
128.B2 Ballets
128.B23 Band music
128.B235 Bandora
128.B24 Baritone. Euphonium
128.B26 Bassoon
128.B29 Big band music
128.B3 Biography
128.B45 Black music. Afro-American music
128.B47 Music for the blind
128.B49 Blues
128.B73 Brass instruments
128.C13 Campaign songs
128.C15 Cantatas
128.C2 Catholic Church music
128.C4 Chamber music
Children's music, see ML128.J8
128.C46 Chorales
128.C48 Choruses
128.C54 Church music
Cf. ML128.C2, Catholic Church music
Cf. ML128.H8, Hymns
Cf. ML128.P7, Protestant church music
Cf. ML128.S17, Sacred music
Cf. ML128.S2, Sacred vocal music
128.C58 Clarinet
128.C59 Community music
Competitions, see ML128.P68
128.C62 Computer music. Computers and music
128.C8 Concertina
128.C84 Concertos
128.C86 Cornett
128.D3 Dance music
128.D56 Discographies
128.D58 Dömbra
128.D6 Double bass
Easter music, see ML128.L2
128.E38 Elche, Festa de
128.E4 Electronic music
English horn, see ML128.O2
128.E8 Ethnomusicology
Euphonium, see ML128.B24
Festa de Elche, see ML128.E38
128.F47 Festivals
128.F7 Flute
128.F74 Folk music
128.F75 Folk songs
128.F8 Funeral music
128.G6 Goigs
128.G74 Ground bass

Bibliography
By topic, A-Z -- Continued

128.G8 Guitar
128.H3 Harp
128.H35 Harpsichord
128.H67 Horn
128.H8 Hymns
128.I6 Incidental music
128.I64 Instruction and study
128.I65 Instrumental music
128.I66 Instruments (General)
128.J3 Jazz
128.J4 Jewish music
128.J8 Juvenile music
128.K37 Karnatic music
128.K5 Keyboard instruments
128.L2 Lenten and Easter music
128.L5 Librettos
128.L88 Lute
128.M2 Madrigals
Cf. ML128.P13, Part-songs
128.M23 Mandolin
128.M25 Marches
128.M27 Medical and physiological aspects of music
128.M3 Medieval music
128.M4 Military music
128.M67 Motets
128.M7 Motion picture music
Music competitions, see ML128.P68
Music theory, see ML128.T5
128.M77 Music therapy
Musical revues, comedies, etc., see ML128.M78
128.M78 Musicals. Revues
128.M8 Musicology
128.N3 National music. Patriotic music
128.N7 Notation
128.O2 Oboe. English horn. Oboe d'amore
Oboe d'amore, see ML128.O2
128.O4 Operas
128.O45 Oratorios
128.O5 Orchestra. Orchestral music
128.O6 Organ
128.P13 Part-songs
Cf. ML128.M2, Madrigals
128.P15 Pastoral music (Secular)
Patriotic music, see ML128.N3
128.P23 Percussion instruments
128.P235 Performance practice
128.P24 Periodicals
128.P26 Peru in music
128.P3 Piano
128.P6 Polonaises
128.P63 Popular music

Bibliography
By topic, A-Z -- Continued
128.P68 Prizes, competitions, etc.
128.P7 Protestant church music
128.R25 Raga
128.R28 Rap
128.R31 Recorder
Revues, see ML128.M78
128.R6 Rock music
128.R65 Rockabilly music
128.S17 Sacred music
128.S2 Sacred vocal music
128.S24 Salsa
128.S247 Saxophone
128.S25 School music
128.S29 Scores
128.S295 Singers
128.S3 Songs
Sound recordings, see ML156+
128.S4 Spirituals
128.S6 Star-spangled banner
128.S7 Stringed instruments
128.S75 Students' songs
128.S9 Symphonies
128.T4 Television music
128.T48 Thematic catalogs
128.T5 Theory, Music
128.T76 Trombone
128.T78 Trumpet
128.T8 Tuba
128.T9 Twelve-tone system
128.V35 Viol
128.V36 Viola
128.V38 Viola d'amore
128.V4 Violin
128.V5 Violoncello
128.V7 Vocal music
128.W2 Wars
128.W4 Wedding music
128.W5 Wind instruments
128.W7 Women in music
128.Z8 Zither
132.A-Z Graded lists. By medium
132.A2 General works
132.B3 Band music
132.C4 Chamber music
132.C5 Choral music
132.H27 Handbell music
132.H3 Harp music
132.O68 Orchestral music
132.O7 Organ music
132.P3 Piano music
132.S6 Songs

Bibliography
Graded lists. By medium -- Continued
132.S8 String orchestra music
132.T76 Trombone music
132.V36 Viola music
132.V4 Violin music
132.V7 Vocal music
134.A-Z Individual composers, A-Z
Under each:
.xA1-.xA39 Thematic catalogs
.xA4-.xZ General. By compiler
134.5.A-Z Other individuals, A-Z
e.g.
134.5.B74 Brecht, Bertolt, 1898-1956
134.5.J4 Joan, of Arc, Saint, 1412-1431
134.5.L45 Lenin, Vladimir Il'ich, 1870-1924
135 Manuscripts
Cf. ML136.A+, Catalogs of public and institutional libraries
Cf. ML138.A+, Catalogs of private collections
Cf. ML152, Catalogs of secondhand dealers
Catalogs
Libraries
Public and institutional
Including descriptive literature on libraries
136.A1 General
Including union catalogs
136.A11-Z Individual libraries and collections. By place, A11-Z
Subarrange by library, institution, person featured, etc.
138.A-Z Private. By name of collection, A-Z
139 Circulating
140 Iconography. Portraits
Including dealers' catalogs
141.A-Z Exhibitions. By city, A-Z
Subarrange by honoree of the exhibition or name of exhibiting institution
Cf. ML462.A+, Catalogs of exhibitions of musical instruments
Publishers
144 General works

Bibliography
Catalogs
Publishers -- Continued
145.A-Z Individual publishers, A-Z
Subarrange under the Cutter for publisher as follows:
.xA3 General
.xB3 Band music
.xB4 Bibliography
.xC5 Choral music
.xI5 Instruction and study
.xI6 Instrumental music
.xO7 Orchestral music
.xP5 Piano music
.xT5 Theater music
.xV6 Vocal music
150 Dealers
152 Secondhand dealers
155 Instruments
Class here trade catalogs
Cf. ML461+, Descriptive catalogs of musical instruments, instrument collections, and exhibitions
Discography
Class here discographies of music sound recordings on discs, tapes, cylinders, etc.
Including reviews, indexes, etc.
For discographies of non-music sound recordings not limited to a topic, see ZA4750
For discographies of non-music sound recordings on special topics, see the topic in classes B-L and N-Z
By source, collection, etc.
156 General trade catalogs
156.2 Other
Class here catalogs of individual record companies, catalogs of sound recordings in individual libraries, collectors' catalogs, etc.
156.4.A-Z By topic, A-Z
American Indian music, see ML156.4.I5
156.4.B3 Band music
156.4.B36 Banjo music
156.4.B5 Big band music
Bluegrass music, see ML156.4.C7
156.4.B6 Blues. Rhythm and blues
156.4.C4 Chamber music
156.4.C5 Children's music
156.4.C54 Christmas music
Church music, see ML156.4.R4
156.4.C6 Clarinet music
156.4.C65 Computer music
156.4.C7 Country music. Bluegrass music

ML

	Bibliography
	Discography
	By topic, A-Z -- Continued
156.4.D3	Dance music
156.4.E4	Electronic music
156.4.E5	Environmental music
156.4.F35	Faust legend in music
156.4.F45	Folk dance music
156.4.F5	Folk music
156.4.F6	Folk songs
156.4.G4	Gay music
156.4.G8	Guitar music
156.4.H3	Harpsichord music
156.4.H7	Horn music
156.4.I5	Indian music (American Indian)
156.4.I58	Instrumental music
156.4.J3	Jazz
156.4.J4	Jewish music
156.4.L2	Labor songs
156.4.M5	Military music
156.4.M6	Motion picture music
	Musical revues, comedies, etc., see ML156.4.M8
156.4.M8	Musicals. Revues
156.4.N3	National music
156.4.N48	New Age music
156.4.O46	Operas
156.4.O5	Orchestral music
156.4.O6	Organ music
156.4.P27	Pasillos
156.4.P4	Percussion music
156.4.P5	Piano music
156.4.P6	Popular music
156.4.R25	Ragtime music
156.4.R34	Recorder music
156.4.R36	Reggae music
156.4.R4	Religious music
	Rhythm and blues, see ML156.4.B6
	Revues, see ML156.4.M8
156.4.R6	Rock music
156.4.S3	Saxophone music
156.4.S4	School music
156.4.S6	Soul music
156.4.S8	Steel band music
	Symphonic music, see ML156.4.O5
156.4.T4	Television music
156.4.T7	Trombone music
156.4.T8	Trumpet music
156.4.V48	Viola music
156.4.V7	Vocal music
156.4.W6	Women musicians
156.4.W63	World music
156.4.W65	World War, 1939-1945
156.5.A-Z	Individual composers, A-Z

Bibliography
  Discography -- Continued
156.7.A-Z Individual performers, A-Z
156.9 Reviews, indexes, etc.
158 Other (not A-Z)
  Including player-piano rolls
Video recordings, films, etc.
  Class here lists and catalogs of musical performances and other music-related recordings on videodisc, videotape, or film
158.4 General works
158.6.A-Z By topic, A-Z
158.6.C66 Conductors
158.6.O6 Operas
158.6.S9 Swing
158.8 Computer software
History and criticism
  For ethnomusicology, see ML3797.6+
  For historiography and musicology, see ML3797+
General works
159 Published through 1800
160 Published 1801-
161 Outlines. Tables. Syllabi
By period
  Ancient
162 General works
  Including non-Western music
164 Mesopotamia and Egypt
166 Jews
  Including literature on music in the Bible
Greece and Rome
167 Collections
  Including sources, documents, essays
Individual authors
  Class here texts with or without commentary
168 Ancient
169 Modern
Medieval. Renaissance
  Including the 16th century
169.8 Periodicals. Societies. Serials
170 Collected works (nonserial)
  Class here sources, documents, essays
171 Written through 1600
  For theoretical treatises written before 1601, see MT5.5
Written 1601-
172 General works
174 Theory
  Class here works about neumes, organum, ligatures, etc.
178 Sacred music
180 Secular music
182 Troubadours. Trouvères

History and criticism
By period
Medieval. Renaissance
Written 1601- -- Continued
183 Meistersinger. Minnesingers
188 Byzantine music
189 Arab music
190 Other (not A-Z)
1601-
193 General works
194 1601-1700
195 1701-1800
196 1801-1900
197 1901-
By region or country
America
198 General works (Table M3)
199 Latin America (Table M3)
North America
200 United States (Table M4)
200.6 World War I, 1914-1918
Including works such as those issued by the Commission on Training Camp Activities of the U.S. Army and Navy, the War Service of the A.L.A., etc.
205 Canada (Table M4)
207.A-Z West Indies
207.A1 General works
207.A2-Z By country, A-Z
e.g.
207.C8 Cuba (Table M8)
207.P8 Puerto Rico (Table M8)
210 Mexico (Table M4)
Central America
220 General works (Table M3)
221 Belize (Table M4)
222 Costa Rica (Table M4)
223 Guatemala (Table M4)
224 Honduras (Table M4)
225 Nicaragua (Table M4)
226 Panama (Table M4)
227 El Salvador (Table M4)
South America
230 General works (Table M3)
231 Argentina (Table M4)
232 Brazil (Table M4)
233 Chile (Table M4)
234 Colombia (Table M4)
235 Ecuador (Table M4)
236 Peru (Table M4)
237 Uruguay (Table M4)
238 Venezuela (Table M4)
239.A-Z Other, A-Z

History and criticism
By region or country
America
South America
Other, A-Z -- Continued
239.B6 Bolivia (Table M8)
239.P3 Paraguay (Table M8)
239.S9 Surinam (Table M8)
Europe
240 General works (Table M3)
246 Austria (Table M4)
247 Czechoslovakia. Czech Republic (Table M4)
248 Hungary (Table M4)
249 Slovakia (Table M4)
Balkan Peninsula
250 General works (Table M3)
252 Bulgaria (Table M4)
254 Greece (Table M4)
258 Romania (Table M4)
260 Yugoslavia (Table M4)
261 Slovenia (Table M4)
262 Croatia (Table M4)
263 Bosnia and Hercegovina (Table M4)
264 Macedonia (Republic) (Table M4)
265 Belgium (Table M4)
Including Netherlands to about 1600
269 Finland (Table M4)
270 France (Table M4)
275 Germany (Table M4)
British Isles
285 General works (Table M3)
286 England (Table M4)
287 Ireland (Table M4)
288 Scotland (Table M4)
289 Wales (Table M4)
290 Italy (Table M4)
295 Netherlands (Table M4)
For Netherlands to about 1600, see ML265
297 Poland (Table M4)
300 Russia. Soviet Union. Russia (Federation) (Table M4)
For former Soviet republics in Asia, see ML330+
Baltic States
302 General works (Table M3)
303 Estonia (Table M4)
304 Latvia (Table M4)
305 Lithuania (Table M4)
308 Ukraine (Table M4)
309.A-Z Other former Soviet republics (Europe), A-Z
309.B4 Belarus (Table M8)
309.M6 Moldova (Table M8)
Scandinavia
310 General works (Table M3)

History and criticism
By region or country
Europe
Scandinavia -- Continued
311 Denmark (Table M4)
312 Norway (Table M4)
313 Sweden (Table M4)
314 Iceland (Table M4)
315 Spain (Table M4)
317 Portugal (Table M4)
320 Switzerland (Table M4)
325.A-Z Other European countries, A-Z
325.L5 Liechtenstein (Table M8)
325.M3 Malta (Table M8)
325.M6 Monaco (Table M8)
325.S2 San Marino (Table M8)
Asia
330 General works (Table M3)
332 Saudi Arabia (Table M4)
334 Armenia (Table M4)
336 China (Table M4)
337 Taiwan (Table M4)
338 India (Table M4)
340 Japan (Table M4)
342 Korea (Table M4)
Including South Korea
343 Korea (North) (Table M4)
344 Iran (Table M4)
345.A-Z Other Asian countries, A-Z
e.g.
345.T8 Turkey (Table M8)
348 Arab countries (Table M3)
Class here general works
Cf. ML189, Works about Arab music to 1600
For music of individual Arab countries, see ML332-345
350 Africa (Table M3)
360 Australia, Oceania, etc. (Table M3)
Biography
Collective
Including letters
385 General works
390 Composers
Performers
394 General works
Instrumentalists
395 General works
396 Organists
397 Pianists
398 Violinists, violoncellists, etc.
Including string quartets, etc.
399 Other instruments
400 Singers

History and criticism
Biography
Collective -- Continued
402 Conductors
403 Theoreticians, historians, critics, etc.
Including librettists
For works on writers of hymn texts, see BV
404 Manufacturers of instruments
Including works about corporate bodies
405 Music publishers, printers, dealers
Including works about corporate bodies
406 Others
Including collectors, managers, etc.
Individual
410.A-Z Composers, A-Z
Including discussions of a composer's compositions from a historical or biographical perspective
For works consisting primarily of analysis of musical compositions, see MT90+
Bach, Johann Sebastian, 1685-1750
410.B1 General works
410.B13 Critical works
410.B14 Family of Johann Sebastian Bach
Beethoven, Ludwig van, 1770-1827
410.B4 General works
410.B42 Critical works
410.B698 Bond, Carrie Jacobs, 1862-1946
410.C4 Chaĭkovskiĭ, Petr Il'ich, 1840-1893
410.C8 Cornelius, Peter, 1824-1874
Jacobs Bond, Carrie, 1862-1946, see ML410.B698
410.R19 Rama Varma Kulasekhara Perumal, Maharaja of Travancore, 1813-1846
410.R85 Rouget de Lisle, Claude Joseph, 1760-1836
410.S15 Saint-Saëns, Camille, 1835-1921
Svātitirunāḷ, 1813-1846, see ML410.R19
Tchaikovsky, Peter Ilich, 1840-1893, see ML410.C4
410.W1-W2 Wagner, Richard, 1813-1883
Writings
Collections
Class here general and complete collections by date of edition
410.W1A1 German
410.W1A105 Translations
Selected works. Special editions
Subarrange by editor, translator or compiler
410.W1A11-W1A119 Posthumous, unpublished, etc., works
Including fragments, sketches, etc.
Prose works
410.W1A12-W1A125 German
410.W1A126-W1A139 Translations

ML

History and criticism
Biography
Individual
Composers, A-Z
Wagner, Richard, 1813-1883
Writings
Selected works.
Special editions -- Continued

(410.W1A14) Poems
See PT2551.W35
For opera librettos, see ML50

410.W1A142-W1A169 Selections. Anthologies. Quotations
Collected quotations from Wagner's writings

410.W1A17-W1A19 Individual operas

410.W1A191-W1A196 By topic

410.W1A197 Indexes to Wagner's works
Class here separately published indexes

Separate works
Class here works printed separately as books or pamphlets
The arrangement below is based on N. Oesterlein, Katalog einer Richard Wagner-Bibliothek
Subarrange by date of edition, including translations
For opera librettos, see ML50

Philosophical, critical, etc., works

410.W1A204 Beethoven, 1870

410.W1A206 Bericht an den Deutschen Wagner-Verein, 1872

410.W1A208 Bericht an ... Ludwig II. von Bayern über eine in München zu errichtende deutsche Musikschule, 1865

410.W1A21 Ein Brief von Richard Wagner über Franz Liszt's Symphonische Dichtungen, 1857

410.W1A212 Das Bühnenfestspielhaus zu Bayreuth, 1873

410.W1A214 Deutsche Kunst und Deutsche Politik, 1868

410.W1A215 Ein deutscher Musiker in Paris

410.W1A216 Herr Eduard Devrient und sein Styl, 1869

410.W1A218 Drei Operndichtungen nebst einer Mittheilung an seine Freunde, 1852

410.W1A22 Das Judenthum in der Musik, 1869

410.W1A222 Die Kunst und die Revolution, 1849

410.W1A224 Das Kunstwerk der Zukunft, 1850

410.W1A226 Lebens-Bericht, 1884
For the 1912 edition, see ML410.W1W122

Mein Leben, 1911, see ML410.W1W14

410.W1A232 Offener Brief an Ernst von Weber, 1880

410.W1A234 Oper und Drama, 1852

410.W1A236 Eine Pilgerfahrt zu Beethoven

History and criticism
Biography
Individual
Composers, A-Z
Wagner, Richard, 1813-1883
Writings
Separate works
Philosophical, critical, etc., works -- Continued

410.W1A238 Religion und Kunst, 1881
410.W1A24 Richard Wagner's Lehr- und Wanderjahre, 1871
410.W1A242 Richard Wagner's Programm zur Neunten Symphonie von Beethoven
410.W1A244 Ein Theater in Zürich, 1851
410.W1A246 Über das Dirigieren, 1869
410.W1A248 Über die Aufführung des Bühnenfestspiels der Ring des Nibelungen, 1871
410.W1A25 Über die Affführung des Tannhäuser, 1852
410.W1A252 Über die Bestimmung der Oper, 1871
410.W1A254 Über Schauspieler und Sänger, 1872
410.W1A256 Was ist deutsch? 1881
410.W1A258 Die Wibelungen, 1850
410.W1A26 Das Wiener Hof-Operntheater, 1863
410.W1A262 Zukunftsmusik, 1861
410.W1A264 Zwei Briefe von Richard Wagner, 1852
410.W1A266 Other
410.W1A267 Speeches, etc.
410.W1A269 Separates of magazine articles not published separately. By date
410.W1A271 Programs. By date
410.W1A273 Other

Dramatic works
410.W1A28 Die Feen, 1888
410.W1A281 Die Fliegende Holländer, 1843
410.W1A282 Iphigenia in Aulis, 1847
410.W1A283 Das Liebesmahl der Apostel, 1843
410.W1A284 Das Liebesverbot oder Die Novize von Palermo, 1911
410.W1A285 Lohengrin, 1850
410.W1A286 Die Meistersinger von Nürnberg, 1862
410.W1A287 Parsifal, 1877
410.W1A288 Rienzi, 1842
Der Ring des Nibelungen
410.W1A289 Der Ring des Nibelungen, 1863
410.W1A29 Das Rheingold, 1869
410.W1A291 Die Walküre, 1870
410.W1A292 Siegfried, 1871
410.W1A293 Götterdämmerung, 1874
410.W1A294 Tannhäuser und der Sängerkrieg auf Wartburg, 1845

History and criticism
Biography
Individual
Composers, A-Z
Wagner, Richard, 1813-1883
Writings
Separate works
Dramatic works -- Continued

410.W1A295 Tristan und Isolde, 1859
410.W1A296 Other
410.W1A298A-Z Parodies, etc. By title, A-Z

Correspondence

410.W1A3-W1A309 General-collected. By date
410.W1A31-W1A319 General-selected. By date
410.W1A32-W1A449 Special-collected. By date
410.W1A45-W1A459 Calendars, etc.
410.W1A47-W1A489 Letters written to Wagner

Biography and criticism
Including autobiographical literature
Biographical works

410.W1A5 Periodicals. Societies. Serials
410.W1A6-W1Z General works
410.W1W122 Lebens-Bericht, 1912
410.W1W14 Mein Leben, 1911
410.W11A-Z Particular periods in the life of Wagner. By author
410.W12A-Z By region or country, A-Z
Class here works about Wagner's influence, Wagner in France, in Italy, etc.

Critical works

410.W13 General works
410.W131 Addresses, essays, lectures

Analytical guides, etc.
Cf. MT100.W2+, Analysis and appreciation of musical works by Wagner

Separate works

410.W132 Early operas
Including Der fliegende Holländer
410.W135 Tannhäuser
410.W137 Lohengrin
410.W14 Tristan und Isolde
410.W15 Ring des Nibelungen
410.W16 Meistersinger
410.W17 Parsifal
410.W175 Other
(410.W18) Literary works
See PT2551.W36
410.W19 Other special
410.W195 Pictorial works
Class here scenes from his operas, etc.
410.W196 Portraits, caricatures, etc.

History and criticism
Biography
Individual
Composers, A-Z
Wagner, Richard, 1813-1883
Biography and criticism
Critical works -- Continued

410.W2 Bayreuth

(410.W203) Literature on Wagner for children
See ML3930.W2

(410.W205) Poems, plays, novels, etc., on Wagner
See subclasses PA-PT

Performers
If a musician is known as both a composer and a performer, classify biographies according to the relative importance of his or her activity in the different fields of music. Where the distinction may not be clear, e.g., Franz Liszt, classify biographies with composers.

Instrumental

416.A-Z Organists, A-Z

416.S33 Schweitzer, Albert, 1875-1965
Cf. B2430.S37, Schweitzer as philosopher
Cf. BX4827.S35, Schweitzer as theologian
Cf. CT1018.S45, Schweitzer (General biography)
Cf. R722.32.S35, Schweitzer as medical missionary

417.A-Z Pianists, A-Z

418.A-Z Violinists, violoncellists, etc., A-Z

419.A-Z Other, A-Z

420.A-Z Vocal, A-Z
e.g.
Chaliapin, Fyodor Ivanovich, see ML420.S53
Del Monaco, Mario, 1915- , see ML420.M557

420.M557 Monaco, Mario del, 1915-

420.R73 Robeson, Paul, 1989-1976

420.S53 Shali͡apin, Feodor Ivanovich, 1873-1938

421.A-Z Vocal and instrumental performing groups, A-Z
e.g.

421.A44 Amadeus String Quartet

421.B4 The Beatles

421.P6 Pink Floyd

421.R64 Rolling Stones

422.A-Z Conductors, A-Z

423.A-Z Theoreticians, historians, critics, etc., A-Z
Including librettists
For works on writers of hymn texts, see BV

423.C55 Chorley, Henry Fothergill, 1808-1872

423.D15 Da Ponte, Lorenzo, 1749-1838

History and criticism
Biography
Individual -- Continued
424.A-Z Manufacturers of instruments, A-Z
Including works about corporate bodies
427.A-Z Music publishers, printers, dealers, A-Z
Including works about corporate bodies
429.A-Z Managers and others, A-Z
Composition
430 General works
430.5 Style
430.7 Improvisation
Notation
431 General works
432 Reform proposals
437 Rhythm
440 Melody
442 Thorough bass
444 Harmony
446 Counterpoint
448 Musical form
Class here works not limited to a specific medium of performance
455 Instrumentation
457 Interpretation. Performance practice
458 Conducting
Instruments and instrumental music
459 Periodicals. Societies. Serials
460 General works
Descriptive catalogs of musical instruments, instrument collections, and exhibitions
For trade catalogs, see ML155
461 General works
462.A-Z Individual collections and exhibitions. By city, A-Z
Subarrange by name of institution
By period
465 Early to 1600
For ancient periods, see ML162+
467 1601-1750
469 1751-1850
471 1851-
By region or country
America
475 General works (Table M3)
476 United States (Table M4)
478 Canada (Table M4)
480 West Indies
Including individual countries (not A-Z)
482 Mexico (Table M4)
484 Central America
Including individual countries (not A-Z)
486.A-Z South America

History and criticism
Instruments and instrumental music
By region or country
America
South America -- Continued
486.A1 General works (Table M7)
486.A7 Argentina (Table M8)
486.B5 Bolivia (Table M8)
486.B7 Brazil (Table M8)
486.C5 Chile (Table M8)
486.C6 Colombia (Table M8)
486.E25 Ecuador (Table M8)
486.P4 Peru (Table M8)
486.V45 Venezuela (Table M8)
Europe
489 General works (Table M3)
491 Austria (Table M4)
493 Czechoslovakia. Czech Republic (Table M4)
494 Hungary (Table M4)
495 Slovakia (Table M4)
496 Belgium (Table M4)
497 France (Table M4)
499 Germany (Table M4)
501 British Isles
Including individual countries (not A-Z)
503 Italy (Table M4)
505 Netherlands (Table M4)
507 Russia. Soviet Union. Russia (Federation) (Table M4)
508.A-Z Baltic States
508.A1 General works (Table M7)
508.E8 Estonia (Table M8)
508.L4 Latvia (Table M8)
508.L6 Lithuania (Table M8)
511.A-Z Other former Soviet republics (Europe), A-Z
For Asian republics, see ML541.A+
511.B4 Belarus (Table M8)
511.M6 Moldova (Table M8)
511.U38 Ukraine (Table M8)
Scandinavia
513 General works (Table M3)
514 Denmark (Table M4)
515 Norway (Table M4)
516 Sweden (Table M4)
518 Spain (Table M4)
519 Portugal (Table M4)
520 Switzerland (Table M4)
522.A-Z Other European countries, A-Z
Asia
525 General works (Table M3)
527 Saudi Arabia (Table M4)
531 China (Table M4)
533 India (Table M4)

ML

History and criticism
Instruments and instrumental music
By region or country
Asia -- Continued
535 Japan (Table M4)
537 Korea (Table M4)
539 Iran (Table M4)
541.A-Z Other Asian regions or countries, A-Z
544 Africa (Table M3)
547 Australia, Oceania, etc. (Table M3)
548 Jews
Instruments
Keyboard instruments
549 General works
Organ
549.8 Periodicals. Societies. Serials
549.9 Congresses
550 General works
Construction
Class here works about history, theory, repair
For tuning, see MT165
552 General works
By period
553 Early to 1600
554 1601-1700
555 1701-1800
556 1801-1900
557 1901-
By region or country
North America
560 General works (Table M3)
561 United States (Table M4)
563 Canada (Table M4)
564 West Indies
Including individual countries (not A-Z)
565 Mexico (Table M4)
567 Central America
Including individual countries (not A-Z)
568 South America
Including individual countries (not A-Z)
Europe
570 General works (Table M3)
572 Austria (Table M4)
573 Belgium (Table M4)
574 France (Table M4)
576 Germany (Table M4)
578 British Isles
Including individual countries (not A-Z)
580 Italy (Table M4)
582 Netherlands (Table M4)

History and criticism
Instruments and instrumental music
Instruments
Keyboard instruments
Organ
Construction
By region or country
Europe -- Continued
584 Russia. Soviet Union. Russia (Federation) (Table M4)
586 Scandinavia
Including individual countries (not A-Z)
588 Spain (Table M4)
589 Portugal (Table M4)
590 Switzerland (Table M4)
592.A-Z Other regions or countries, A-Z
Class here European and other regions or countries
Individual organs
Including history and specifications
594.A1 Collected works (nonserial)
594.A3-Z By place, A-Z
595 Special parts of the organ
597 Reed organs and other special kinds of organ
Music and playing
600 General works
By period
603 Early to 1600
604 1601-1700
605 1701-1800
606 1801-1900
607 1901-
By region or country
North America
610 General works (Table M3)
611 United States (Table M4)
613 Canada (Table M4)
614 West Indies
Including individual countries (not A-Z)
615 Mexico (Table M4)
617 Central America
Including individual countries (not A-Z)
618 South America
Including individual countries (not A-Z)
Europe
620 General works (Table M3)
622 Austria (Table M4)
623 Belgium (Table M4)
624 France (Table M4)
626 Germany (Table M4)

History and criticism
Instruments and instrumental music
Instruments
Keyboard instruments
Organ
Music and playing
By region or country
Europe -- Continued
628 British Isles
Including individual countries (not A-Z)
630 Italy (Table M4)
632 Netherlands (Table M4)
634 Russia. Soviet Union. Russia (Federation) (Table M4)
636 Scandinavia
Including individual countries (not A-Z)
638 Spain (Table M4)
639 Portugal (Table M4)
640 Switzerland (Table M4)
642.A-Z Other regions or countries, A-Z
Class here European and other regions or countries
Forms and types
645 Sonata
646 Suite
647 Other (not A-Z)
649 Reed organ music
Piano, clavichord, harpsichord, etc.
Class here works about the piano or its predecessors
649.8 Periodicals. Societies. Serials
650 General works
651 Predecessors of the piano
Construction
Class here works about history, theory, repair
652 General works
By period
653 Early to 1600
654 1601-1700
655 1701-1800
656 1801-1900
657 1901-
By region or country
North America
660 General works (Table M3)
661 United States (Table M4)
663 Canada (Table M4)
664 West Indies
Including individual countries (not A-Z)

History and criticism
Instruments and instrumental music
Instruments
Keyboard instruments
Piano, clavichord, harpsichord, etc.
Construction
By region or country
North America -- Continued
665 Mexico (Table M4)
667 Central America
Including individual countries (not A-Z)
668 South America
Including individual countries (not A-Z)
Europe
670 General works (Table M3)
672 Austria (Table M4)
673 Belgium (Table M4)
674 France (Table M4)
676 Germany (Table M4)
678 British Isles
Including individual countries (not A-Z)
680 Italy (Table M4)
682 Netherlands (Table M4)
684 Russia. Soviet Union. Russia (Federation) (Table M4)
686 Scandinavia
Including individual countries (not A-Z)
688 Spain (Table M4)
689 Portugal (Table M4)
690 Switzerland (Table M4)
692.A-Z Other regions or countries, A-Z
Class here European and other regions or countries
694 Special makes
Cf. ML424.A+, Individual manufacturers of instruments
695 Special parts of the piano
697 Other kinds of pianos
Including new keyboards and electronic pianos
Music and playing
700 General works
By period
703 Early to 1600
704 1601-1700
705 1701-1800
706 1801-1900
707 1901-
By region or country
North America
710 General works (Table M3)

History and criticism
Instruments and instrumental music
Instruments
Keyboard instruments
Piano, clavichord, harpsichord, etc.
Music and playing
By region or country
North America -- Continued
711 United States (Table M4)
713 Canada (Table M4)
714 West Indies
Including individual countries (not A-Z)
715 Mexico (Table M4)
717 Central America
Including individual countries (not A-Z)
718 South America
Including individual countries (not A-Z)
Europe
720 General works (Table M3)
722 Austria (Table M4)
723 Belgium (Table M4)
724 France (Table M4)
726 Germany (Table M4)
728 British Isles
Including individual countries (not A-Z)
730 Italy (Table M4)
732 Netherlands (Table M4)
734 Russia. Soviet Union. Russia (Federation) (Table M4)
736 Scandinavia
Including individual countries (not A-Z)
738 Spain (Table M4)
739 Portugal (Table M4)
740 Switzerland (Table M4)
742.A-Z Other regions or countries, A-Z
Class here European and other regions or countries
Forms and types
745 Sonata
746 Suite
747 Other (not A-Z)
Bowed stringed instruments
749.5 Periodicals. Societies. Serials
750 General works
755 Construction
Class here works about history, theory, repair
756 Music and playing
(760) Early instruments
See ML927
Violin

History and criticism
Instruments and instrumental music
Instruments
Bowed stringed instruments
Violin -- Continued
800 General works
Construction
Class here works about history, theory, repair
802 General works
By period
803 Early to 1600
804 1601-1700
805 1701-1800
806 1801-1900
807 1901-
By region or country
North America
810 General works (Table M3)
811 United States (Table M4)
813 Canada (Table M4)
814 West Indies
Including individual countries (not A-Z)
815 Mexico (Table M4)
817 Central America
Including individual countries (not A-Z)
818 South America
Including individual countries (not A-Z)
Europe
820 General works (Table M3)
822 Austria (Table M4)
823 Belgium (Table M4)
824 France (Table M4)
826 Germany (Table M4)
828 British Isles
Including individual countries (not A-Z)
830 Italy (Table M4)
832 Netherlands (Table M4)
834 Russia. Soviet Union. Russia (Federation) (Table M4)
836 Scandinavia
Including individual countries (not A-Z)
838 Spain (Table M4)
839 Portugal (Table M4)
840 Switzerland (Table M4)
842.A-Z Other regions or countries, A-Z
Class here European and other regions or countries
845 Special parts of the violin
Including the bow

History and criticism
Instruments and instrumental music
Instruments
Bowed stringed instruments
Violin
Construction -- Continued
846 Other
Class here books on prices of violins, etc.
Music and playing
850 General works
By period
853 Early to 1600
854 1601-1700
855 1701-1800
856 1801-1900
857 1901-
By region or country
North America
860 General works (Table M3)
861 United States (Table M4)
863 Canada (Table M4)
864 West Indies
Including individual countries (not A-Z)
865 Mexico (Table M4)
867 Central America
Including individual countries (not A-Z)
868 South America
Including individual countries (not A-Z)
Europe
870 General works (Table M3)
872 Austria (Table M4)
873 Belgium (Table M4)
874 France (Table M4)
876 Germany (Table M4)
878 British Isles
Including individual countries (not A-Z)
880 Italy (Table M4)
882 Netherlands (Table M4)
884 Russia. Soviet Union. Russia (Federation) (Table M4)
886 Scandinavia
Including individual countries (not A-Z)
888 Spain (Table M4)
889 Portugal (Table M4)
890 Switzerland (Table M4)
892.A-Z Other regions or countries, A-Z
Class here European and other regions or countries
Forms and types

History and criticism
Instruments and instrumental music
Instruments
Bowed stringed instruments
Violin
Music and playing
Forms and types -- Continued
895 Sonata
896 Suite
897 Other (not A-Z)
Viola
900 General works
901 Construction
905 Music and playing
Violoncello
910 General works
911 Construction
915 Music and playing
Double bass
920 General works
921 Construction
925 Music and playing
927.A-Z Other bowed stringed instruments, A-Z
927.C36 Campanula
927.G83 Gŭdulka
927.H27 Hardanger fiddle
927.K49 Keyed fiddle
927.L57 Lira da braccio
927.L9 Lyra
927.L97 Lyra viol
927.P75 Psalmodikon
927.R33 Rabāb
927.S4 Sarangi
927.T7 Trumpet marine
927.V5 Viol
927.V6 Violo
927.V63 Violone
Wind instruments
929 Periodicals. Societies. Serials
929.5 Congresses
930 General works
931 Woodwind instruments (General)
933 Brass instruments (General)
Flute. Piccolo
935 General works
936 Construction
937 Music and playing
Oboe
940 General works
941 Construction
943 Music and playing
Clarinet
945 General works

History and criticism
Instruments and instrumental music
Instruments
Wind instruments
Clarinet -- Continued
946 Construction
948 Music and playing
Bassoon
950 General works
951 Construction
953 Music and playing
Horn
955 General works
956 Construction
958 Music and playing
Trumpet. Cornet
960 General works
961 Construction
963 Music and playing
Trombone
965 General works
966 Construction
968 Music and playing
Tuba. Baritone, etc.
970 General works
971 Construction
973 Music and playing
Saxophone
975 General works
976 Construction
978 Music and playing
980 Bagpipes
990.A-Z Other wind instruments, A-Z
990.A5 Alboka
990.B32 Bānsurī
990.B35 Basset horn
990.C5 Chalumeau
990.C65 Cornett
(990.C68) Courting flute
See ML990.N37
990.C8 Crumhorn
990.C95 Czakan
990.D53 Didjeridu
990.D8 Dulzaina
990.F6 Flaviol
990.H4 Heckelphone
990.H75 Hsiao
990.K36 Kaval
990.L57 Liquimofono
990.N37 Native American flute
990.N39 Nāy
990.O3 Ocarina
990.O7 Ophicleide

History and criticism
Instruments and instrumental music
Instruments
Wind instruments
Other wind instruments, A-Z -- Continued

990.P45 Penny whistle
990.P67 Post horn
990.Q46 Quena
990.R4 Recorder
990.R8 Russian horn
990.S3 Sackbut
990.S5 Shakuhachi
Sheng, see ML1089.S5
990.S55 Shofar
990.S58 Siku
990.S6 Siwa
990.Z8 Zumari

Plucked instruments
999 Periodicals. Societies. Serials
1000 General works
1001 Construction
1003 Music and playing
Harp
1005 General works
1006 Construction
1008 Music and playing
Lute
1010 General works
1011 Construction
Music and playing
1012 Sources, documents, etc.
Class here early literature to about 1650
1013 Modern authors
1015.A-Z Other instruments, A-Z
1015.A6 Appalachian dulcimer
1015.A9 Autoharp
1015.B23 Bağlama
1015.B24 Balalaika
1015.B25 Bandura
1015.B26 Bandurria
1015.B3 Banjo
1015.B4 Berimbau
1015.B55 Biwa
1015.C3 Celtic harp
1015.C37 Charango
1015.C47 Cheng
1015.C5 Ch'in
1015.C83 Cuatro
Dulcimer, see ML1041
Dulcimer, Appalachian, see ML1015.A6
1015.G9 Guitar
1015.G93 Gusli
1015.I3 Ichigenkin

History and criticism
Instruments and instrumental music
Instruments
Plucked instruments
Other instruments, A-Z -- Continued

1015.K23 Kacapi (Lute)
1015.K3 Kantele
1015.K6 Kobza
1015.K64 Kokle
1015.K68 Koto
1015.L89 Lyre
1015.L9 Lyre-guitar
1015.M2 Mandolin
1015.M25 Mbira
1015.O9 Oud
1015.P5 P'i p'a
1015.P8 Psaltery
1015.S3 San hsien
1015.S35 Sanza
1015.S37 Sarod
1015.S4 Saz
1015.S52 Shamisen
1015.S6 Sitar
1015.T3 Tambura
1015.T5 Tiple
1015.U5 Ukulele
1015.V5 Vina
1015.V56 Viola-de-cocho
1015.Y83 Yüeh ch'in
1015.Z5 Zither

Percussion instruments
1030 General works
Drum(s)
Including drum set
1035 General works
1036 Timpani
1038.A-Z Other, A-Z
1038.A7 Arará
1038.A8 Atabaque
1038.B38 Batá
1038.B63 Bodhrán
1038.B66 Bonkó
1038.B7 Bronze drum
1038.C4 Cenḍa
1038.D5 Dhimay
1038.K7 Kotsuzumi
1038.M74 Mridanga
1038.N4 Nāykhīm
1038.P85 Pung
1038.R43 Rebana
1038.S26 Santūr
1038.S74 Steel drum
1038.T3 Tabla

History and criticism
Instruments and instrumental music
Instruments
Percussion instruments
Drum(s)
Other, A-Z -- Continued
1038.T85 Tupan
1039 Bells. Carillons. Gongs. Chimes
Including change ringing, peals, etc.
1041 Dulcimer
1048 Xylophone and similar instruments
Including marimba, vibraphone, anklung, etc.
1049 Other percussion instruments (not A-Z)
Mechanical instruments, devices, etc.
1049.8 Periodicals. Societies. Serials
1050 General works
1055 Phonograph. Sound recordings. Music recorders
1058 Barrel organ. Mechanical organs
Music box
1065 Periodicals. Societies. Serials
1066 General works
1067 Musical clocks
1070 Player-piano and similar instruments
1080 Metronome
1081 Other (not A-Z)
Other instruments
1083 Accordion. Bandonion. Concertina
1085 Glass harmonica
1086 Hurdy-gurdy
1087 Jew's harp
Mouth organs
1088 Harmonica
1089.A-Z Other, A-Z
1089.K24 Kaen
1089.M45 Melodica
1089.S5 Sheng
1089.S54 Shō
1091 Other (not A-Z)
Electronic instruments
1091.8 Periodicals. Societies. Serials
1092 General works
1093 Computers as musical instruments
For general works on the use of computers in the field of music, see ML74
Ensembles
Chamber music
1100 General works
By period
1102 Early to 1750
1104 1751-1900
1106 1901-
By region or country
North America

History and criticism
Instruments and instrumental music
Ensembles
Chamber music
By region or country
North America -- Continued
1110 General works (Table M3)
1111 United States (Table M4)
1113 Canada (Table M4)
1114 West Indies
Including individual countries (not A-Z)
1115 Mexico (Table M4)
1117 Central America
Including individual countries (not A-Z)
1118 South America
Including individual countries (not A-Z)
Europe
1120 General works (Table M3)
1122 Austria (Table M4)
1126 Belgium (Table M4)
1127 France (Table M4)
1129 Germany (Table M4)
1131 British Isles
Including individual countries (not A-Z)
1133 Italy (Table M4)
1135 Netherlands (Table M4)
1137 Russia. Soviet Union. Russia (Federation) (Table M4)
1142 Scandinavia
Including individual countries (not A-Z)
1147 Spain (Table M4)
1148 Portugal (Table M4)
1149 Switzerland (Table M4)
1151.A-Z Other regions or countries, A-Z
Class here European and other regions or countries
Forms and types
1156 Sonata
1158 Suite
1160 String quartet
1165 Other (not A-Z)
Orchestra
For dance orchestra music, see ML3518
1200 General works
By period
1202 Early to 1750
1204 1751-1850
1206 1851-1950
1208 1951-
By region or country
North America
1210 General works (Table M3)
1211 United States (Table M4)

History and criticism
Instruments and instrumental music
Ensembles
Orchestra
By region or country
North America -- Continued
1213 Canada (Table M4)
1214 West Indies
Including individual countries (not A-Z)
1215 Mexico (Table M4)
1216 Central America
Including individual countries (not A-Z)
1217 South America
Including individual countries (not A-Z)
Europe
1220 General works (Table M3)
1222 Austria (Table M4)
1226 Belgium (Table M4)
1227 France (Table M4)
1229 Germany (Table M4)
1231 British Isles
Including individual countries (not A-Z)
1233 Italy (Table M4)
1235 Netherlands (Table M4)
1237 Russia. Soviet Union. Russia (Federation) (Table M4)
1242 Scandinavia
Including individual countries (not A-Z)
1247 Spain (Table M4)
1248 Portugal (Table M4)
1249 Switzerland (Table M4)
1251.A-Z Other regions or countries, A-Z
Class here European and other regions or countries
Forms and types
1255 Symphony
1258 Suite
1261 Overture
1263 Concerto
1270.A-Z Other forms, A-Z
e.g.
1270.S9 Symphonic poem
Band
Including military music
For big band, jazz band, dance band, or dance orchestra music, see ML3518
1299 Periodicals. Societies. Serials
1300 General works
By period
1302 Early to 1800
1304 1801-1900
1306 1901-
By region or country

History and criticism
Instruments and instrumental music
Ensembles
Band
By region or country -- Continued
North America
1310 General works (Table M3)
1311 United States (Table M4)
1313 Canada (Table M4)
1314 West Indies
Including individual countries (not A-Z)
1315 Mexico (Table M4)
1316 Central America
Including individual countries (not A-Z)
1317 South America
Including individual countries (not A-Z)
Europe
1320 General works (Table M3)
1322 Austria (Table M4)
1326 Belgium (Table M4)
1327 France (Table M4)
1329 Germany (Table M4)
1331 British Isles
Including individual countries (not A-Z)
1333 Italy (Table M4)
1335 Netherlands (Table M4)
1337 Russia. Soviet Union. Russia (Federation) (Table M4)
1342 Scandinavia
Including individual countries (not A-Z)
1347 Spain (Table M4)
1348 Portugal (Table M4)
1349 Switzerland (Table M4)
1351.A-Z Other regions or countries, A-Z
Class here European and other regions or countries
1354 Forms and types
Electronic music. Computer music
For general works on the use of computers in the field of music, see ML74
1379 Periodicals. Societies. Serials
1380 General works
Vocal music
1400 General works
By period
1402 Early to 1600
1403 1601-1700
1404 1701-1800
1405 1801-1900
1406 1901-
By region or country
North America
1410 General works (Table M3)

History and criticism
Vocal music
By region or country
North America -- Continued
1411 United States (Table M4)
1413 Canada (Table M4)
1414 West Indies
Including individual countries (not A-Z)
1415 Mexico (Table M4)
1416 Central America
Including individual countries (not A-Z)
1417 South America
Including individual countries (not A-Z)
Europe
1420 General (Table M3)
1422 Austria (Table M4)
1424 Czechoslovakia. Czech Republic (Table M4)
1425 Hungary (Table M4)
1426 Belgium (Table M4)
1427 France (Table M4)
1429 Germany (Table M4)
1431 British Isles
Including individual countries (not A-Z)
1433 Italy (Table M4)
1435 Netherlands (Table M4)
1437 Russia. Soviet Union. Russia (Federation) (Table M4)
1440 Poland (Table M4)
1442 Scandinavia
Including individual countries (not A-Z)
1446 Slovakia (Table M4)
1447 Spain (Table M4)
1448 Portugal (Table M4)
1449 Switzerland (Table M4)
1451.A-Z Other regions or countries, A-Z
Class here European and other regions or countries
1460 Vocal technique
Cf. MT823, History of vocal instruction and study
Choral music
Including sacred and secular music
1499 Periodicals. Societies. Serials
1500 General works
By period
1502 Early to 1600
1503 1601-1700
1504 1701-1800
1505 1801-1900
1506 1901-
By region or country
North America
1510 General works (Table M3)

ML

History and criticism
Vocal music
Choral music
By region or country
North America -- Continued
1511 United States (Table M4)
1513 Canada (Table M4)
1514 West Indies
Including individual countries (not A-Z)
1515 Mexico (Table M4)
1516 Central America
Including individual countries (not A-Z)
1517 South America
Including individual countries (not A-Z)
Europe
1520 General works (Table M3)
1522 Austria (Table M4)
1526 Belgium (Table M4)
1527 France (Table M4)
1528 Germany (Table M4)
1531 British Isles
Including individual countries (not A-Z)
1533 Italy (Table M4)
1535 Netherlands (Table M4)
1537 Russia. Soviet Union. Russia (Federation) (Table M4)
1542 Scandinavia
Including individual countries (not A-Z)
1547 Spain (Table M4)
1548 Portugal (Table M4)
1549 Switzerland (Table M4)
1551.A-Z Other regions or countries, A-Z
Class here European and other regions or countries
1554 Forms and types
Class here works about both sacred and secular music
Secular vocal music
1600 General works
By period
1602 Early to 1600
1603 1601-1700
1604 1701-1800
1605 1801-1900
1606 1901-
By region or country
North America
1610 General works (Table M3)
1611 United States (Table M4)
1613 Canada (Table M4)
1614 West Indies
Including individual countries (not A-Z)
1615 Mexico (Table M4)

History and criticism
Vocal music
Secular vocal music
By region or country -- Continued
1616 Central America
Including individual countries (not A-Z)
1617 South America
Including individual countries (not A-Z)
Europe
1620 General works (Table M3)
1622 Austria
1626 Belgium (Table M4)
1627 France (Table M4)
1629 Germany (Table M4)
1631 British Isles
Including individual countries (not A-Z)
1633 Italy (Table M4)
1635 Netherlands (Table M4)
1637 Russia. Soviet Union. Russia (Federation) (Table M4)
1642 Scandinavia
Including individual countries (not A-Z)
1647 Spain (Table M4)
1648 Portugal (Table M4)
1649 Switzerland (Table M4)
1651.A-Z Other regions or countries, A-Z
Class here European and other regions or countries
Forms and types
Dramatic music
Class here works about opera, incidental music, melodrama, etc.
For works about ballet, pantomime, etc., music, see ML3460
1699 Periodicals. Societies. Serials
1700 General works
1700.1 Addresses, essays, lectures
By period
1702 Early to 1650
1703 1651-1750
1704 1751-1850
1705 1851-1950
1706 1951-
By region or country
North America
1710 General works (Table M3)
1711 United States (Table M4)
1713 Canada (Table M4)
1714 West Indies
Including individual countries (not A-Z)
1715 Mexico (Table M4)
1716 Central America
Including individual countries (not A-Z)

History and criticism
Vocal music
Secular vocal music
Forms and types
Dramatic music
By region or country -- Continued
1717 South America
Including individual countries (not A-Z)
Europe
1720 General works (Table M3)
1723 Austria (Table M4)
1724 Czechoslovakia. Czech Republic (Table M4)
1725 Hungary (Table M4)
1726 Belgium (Table M4)
France
1727 General works (Table M4)
1727.33 Guerre des bouffons
Class sources here
1727.35 Gluck-Piccinni controversy
Class sources here
1729 Germany (Table M4)
1731 British Isles
Including individual countries (not A-Z)
1733 Italy (Table M4)
1735 Netherlands (Table M4)
1736 Poland (Table M4)
1737 Russia. Soviet Union. Russia (Federation) (Table M4)
1738.A-Z Baltic States
1738.A1 General works
1738.E8 Estonia (Table M8)
1738.L4 Latvia (Table M8)
1738.L5 Lithuania (Table M8)
1741.A-Z Other former Soviet republics (Europe), A-Z
For Asian republics, see ML1751.A+
1741.B4 Belarus (Table M8)
1741.M6 Moldava (Table M8)
1741.U78 Ukraine (Table M8)
Scandinavia
1742 General works (Table M3)
1743 Denmark (Table M4)
1744 Norway (Table M4)
1745 Sweden (Table M4)
1746 Slovakia (Table M4)
1747 Spain (Table M4)
1748 Portugal (Table M4)
1749 Switzerland (Table M4)
1751.A-Z Other regions or countries, A-Z
Class here European and other regions or countries

History and criticism
Vocal music
Secular vocal music
Forms and types
Dramatic music -- Continued
Forms and types
For works on a particular form or type in a particular country, see the country
1800 Serious opera
1850 Comic opera
1900 Operetta
1950 Other types with spoken dialogue
Class here general works about individual types, e.g., ballad opera, Singspiel, zarzuela
2000 Incidental music
2050 Melodrama
Motion picture music
For works about musical films, see PN1995.9.M86
2074 Periodicals. Societies. Serials
2075 General works
2080 Television music
Cf. PN1992.8.M87, Music videos
2100 Other (not A-Z)
Class here general and special works
Including Faust legend in opera
2110 Libretto writing, translating of librettos, etc.
2400 Cantatas
Class here works on cantatas that include chorus
For works on the solo cantata, see ML2800+
Songs
Class here works about both part-songs and solo songs
For works about part-songs only, see ML2600+
For works about solo songs only, see ML2800+
2500 General works
By period
2502 Early to 1600
2503 1601-1700
2504 1701-1800
2505 1801-1900
2506 1901-
By region or country
North America
2510 General works (Table M3)
2511 United States (Table M4)
2513 Canada (Table M4)
2514 West Indies
Including individual countries (not A-Z)
2515 Mexico (Table M4)

History and criticism
Vocal music
Secular vocal music
Forms and types
Songs
By region or country -- Continued
2516 Central America
Including individual countries (not A-Z)
2517 South America
Including individual countries (not A-Z)
Europe
2520 General works (Table M3)
2522 Austria (Table M4)
2526 Belgium (Table M4)
2527 France (Table M4)
2529 Germany (Table M4)
2531 British Isles
Including individual countries (not A-Z)
2533 Italy (Table M4)
2535 Netherlands (Table M4)
2537 Russia. Soviet Union. Russia (Federation) (Table M4)
2542 Scandinavia
Including individual countries (not A-Z)
2547 Spain (Table M4)
2548 Portugal (Table M4)
2549 Switzerland (Table M4)
2551.A-Z Other regions or countries, A-Z
Class here European and other regions or countries
Part-songs
2600 General works
By period
2602 Early to 1600
2603 1601-1700
2604 1701-1800
2605 1801-1900
2606 1901-
By region or country
North America
2610 General works (Table M3)
2611 United States (Table M4)
2613 Canada (Table M4)
2614 West Indies
Including individual countries (not A-Z)
2615 Mexico (Table M4)
2616 Central America
Including individual countries (not A-Z)
2617 South America
Including individual countries (not A-Z)
Europe
2620 General works (Table M3)

History and criticism
Vocal music
Secular vocal music
Forms and types
Songs
Part-songs
By region or country
Europe -- Continued
2622 Austria (Table M4)
2626 Belgium (Table M4)
2627 France (Table M4)
2629 Germany (Table M4)
2631 British Isles
Including individual countries (not A-Z)
2633 Italy (Table M4)
2635 Netherlands (Table M4)
2637 Russia. Soviet Union. Russia (Federation) (Table M4)
2642 Scandinavia
Including individual countries (not A-Z)
2647 Spain (Table M4)
2648 Portugal (Table M4)
2649 Switzerland (Table M4)
2651.A-Z Other regions or countries, A-Z
Class here European and other regions or countries
Forms and types
2660 Men's voices
2665 Treble voices
2670 Glees, catches, etc.
Solo songs
Class here works about lied, chanson, romance, solo cantata, ballad, aria, etc.
2800 General works
By period
2802 Early to 1600
2803 1601-1750
2804 1751-1800
2805 1801-1850
2806 1851-1900
2807 1901-
By region or country
North America
2810 General works (Table M3)
2811 United States (Table M4)
2813 Canada (Table M4)
2814 West Indies
Including individual countries (not A-Z)
2815 Mexico (Table M4)

History and criticism
Vocal music
Secular vocal music
Forms and types
Songs
Solo songs
By region or country -- Continued
2816 Central America
Including individual countries (not A-Z)
2817 South America
Including individual countries (not A-Z)
Europe
2820 General works (Table M3)
2822 Austria (Table M4)
2826 Belgium (Table M4)
2827 France (Table M4)
2829 Germany (Table M4)
2831 British Isles
Including individual countries (not A-Z)
2833 Italy (Table M4)
2835 Netherlands (Table M4)
2837 Russia. Soviet Union. Russia (Federation) (Table M4)
2842 Scandinavia
Including individual countries (not A-Z)
2847 Spain (Table M4)
2848 Portugal (Table M4)
2849 Switzerland (Table M4)
2851.A-Z Other regions or countries, A-Z
Class here European and other regions or countries
2854 Forms and types
2870 Minstrels (Modern)
Christmas carols
2880 General works
2881.A-Z By region or country, A-Z
Sacred vocal music
2900 General works
By period
2902 Early to 1600
2903 1601-1700
2904 1701-1800
2905 1801-1900
2906 1901-
By region or country
North America
2910 General works (Table M3)
2911 United States (Table M4)
2913 Canada (Table M4)
2914 West Indies
Including individual countries (not A-Z)

History and criticism
Vocal music
Sacred vocal music
By region or country
North America -- Continued
2915 Mexico (Table M4)
2916 Central America
Including individual countries (not A-Z)
2917 South America
Including individual countries (not A-Z)
Europe
2920 General works (Table M3)
2922 Austria (Table M4)
2926 Belgium (Table M4)
2927 France (Table M4)
2929 Germany (Table M4)
2931 British Isles
Including individual countries (not A-Z)
2933 Italy (Table M4)
2935 Netherlands (Table M4)
2937 Russia. Soviet Union. Russia (Federation) (Table M4)
2942 Scandinavia
Including individual countries (not A-Z)
2947 Spain (Table M4)
2948 Portugal (Table M4)
2949 Switzerland (Table M4)
2951.A-Z Other regions or countries, A-Z
Class here European and other regions or countries
Individual religions and denominations
2999 Periodicals. Societies. Serials
3000 General (Christian)
3001 Music in the church
Roman Catholic
3002 General works
By period
3003 Early to 1600
3004 1601-1700
3005 1701-1800
3006 1801-1900
3007 1901-
By region or country
North America
3010 General works (Table M3)
3011 United States (Table M4)
3013 Canada (Table M4)
3014 West Indies
Including individual countries (not A-Z)
3015 Mexico (Table M4)
3016 Central America
Including individual countries (not A-Z)

History and criticism
Vocal music
Sacred vocal music
Individual religions and denominations
Roman Catholic
By region or country -- Continued
3017 South America
Including individual countries (not A-Z)
Europe
3020 General works (Table M3)
3022 Austria (Table M4)
3026 Belgium (Table M4)
3027 France (Table M4)
3029 Germany (Table M4)
3031 British Isles
Including individual countries (not A-Z)
3033 Italy (Table M4)
3036 Netherlands (Table M4)
3037 Russia. Soviet Union. Russia (Federation) (Table M4)
3042 Scandinavia
Including individual countries (not A-Z)
3047 Spain (Table M4)
3048 Portugal (Table M4)
3049 Switzerland (Table M4)
3051.A-Z Other regions or countries, A-Z
Class here European and other regions or countries
Orthodox and other Catholic
3060 Orthodox
3065 Old Catholic
3070 Other (not A-Z)
Forms and types
3080 Liturgy and ritual
3082 Chants (plain, Gregorian, etc.)
3084 Chorale
3086 Psalmody, hymnology, etc.
For works about texts or the origin and meaning of hymns, see BV
3088 Mass
Including Requiem Mass
3090 Individual texts
Including Stabat Mater, Te Deum, etc.
3093 Other
3095 Official instructions, precepts, etc. By date
Protestant
3100 General works
By period
3102 Early to 1600
3103 1601-1700
3104 1701-1800
3105 1801-1900
3106 1901-

History and criticism
Vocal music
Sacred vocal music
Individual religions and denominations
Protestant -- Continued
By region or country
North America
3110 General works (Table M3)
3111 United States (Table M4)
3113 Canada (Table M4)
3114 West Indies
Including individual countries (not A-Z)
3115 Mexico (Table M4)
3116 Central America
Including individual countries (not A-Z)
3117 South America
Including individual countries (not A-Z)
Europe
3120 General works (Table M3)
3122 Austria (Table M4)
3126 Belgium (Table M4)
3127 France (Table M4)
3129 Germany
3131 British Isles
Including individual countries (not A-Z)
3133 Italy (Table M4)
3135 Netherlands (Table M4)
3137 Finland (Table M4)
3142 Scandinavia
Including individual countries (not A-Z)
3147 Spain (Table M4)
3148 Portugal (Table M4)
3149 Switzerland (Table M4)
3151.A-Z Other regions or countries, A-Z
Class here European and other regions or countries
By denomination
3160 Baptist
3161 Church of the Brethren
3161.5 Christian Science. Church of Christ, Scientist
3162 Congregational
3164 Dutch and other Reformed
3166 Anglican Communion
3167 Evangelical and Reformed Church
3167.5 Society of Friends (Quakers)
3168 Lutheran
3169 Mennonite
3170 Methodist
3172 Moravian
3174 Mormon. Church of Jesus Christ of Latter-day Saints
3176 Presbyterian

History and criticism
Vocal music
Sacred vocal music
Individual religions and denominations
Protestant
By denomination -- Continued
3178.A-Z Other, A-Z
Forms and types
3182 Liturgy and ritual
3184 Chorale
3186 Psalmody, hymnology, etc.
For works about texts or the origin and meaning of hymns, see BV
Gospel music
3186.8 Periodicals. Societies. Serials
3187 General works
3187.5 Contemporary Christian music
Including Christian rock music
3188 Other (not A-Z)
3190 Other Christian denominations
3195 Jewish
3197 Other religions (not A-Z)
Including Islamic
Forms and types
Oratorio
3201 General works
By period
3203 Early to 1600
3204 1601-1700
3205 1701-1800
3206 1801-1900
3207 1901-
By region or country
North America
3210 General works (Table M3)
3211 United States (Table M4)
3213 Canada (Table M4)
3214 West Indies
Including individual countries (not A-Z)
3215 Mexico (Table M4)
3216 Central America
Including individual countries (not A-Z)
3217 South America
Including individual countries (not A-Z)
Europe
3220 General works (Table M3)
3222 Austria (Table M4)
3226 Belgium (Table M4)
3227 France (Table M4)
3229 Germany (Table M4)
3231 British Isles
Including individual countries (not A-Z)
3233 Italy (Table M4)

History and criticism
Vocal music
Sacred vocal music
Forms and types
Oratorio
By region or country
Europe -- Continued

3235 Netherlands (Table M4)
3237 Russia. Soviet Union. Russia (Federation) (Table M4)
3242 Scandinavia
Including individual countries (not A-Z)
3247 Spain (Table M4)
3248 Portugal (Table M4)
3249 Switzerland (Table M4)
3251.A-Z Other regions or countries, A-Z
Class here European and other regions or countries
3260 Cantatas and similar sacred works
3265 Chorales
Class here works not treated from a denominational standpoint
3270 Church songs
Class here works about psalmody, hymnology, etc., if not treated from a denominational standpoint
3275 Other (not A-Z)

Program music
3300 General works
By period
3302 Early to 1800
3303 1801-1900
3304 1901-
By region or country
North America
3310 General works (Table M3)
3311 United States (Table M4)
3313 Canada (Table M4)
3314 West Indies
Including individual countries (not A-Z)
3315 Mexico (Table M4)
3316 Central America
Including individual countries (not A-Z)
3317 South America
Including individual countries (not A-Z)
Europe
3320 General works (Table M3)
3322 Austria (Table M4)
3326 Belgium (Table M4)
3327 France (Table M4)
3329 Germany (Table M4)
3331 British Isles
Including individual countries (not A-Z)

ML

History and criticism
Program music
By region or country
Europe -- Continued
3333 Italy (Table M4)
3335 Netherlands (Table M4)
3337 Russia. Soviet Union. Russia (Federation) (Table M4)
3342 Scandinavia
Including individual countries (not A-Z)
3347 Spain (Table M4)
3348 Portugal (Table M4)
3349 Switzerland (Table M4)
3351.A-Z Other regions or countries, A-Z
Class here European and other regions or countries
3354.A-Z Forms and types, A-Z
Dance music
For history of dancing, see GV1580+
3400 General works
By period
3402 Early to 1600
3403 1601-1700
3404 1701-1800
3405 1801-1900
3406 1901-
By region or country
North America
3410 General works (Table M3)
3411 United States (Table M4)
3413 Canada (Table M4)
3414 West Indies
Including individual countries (not A-Z)
3415 Mexico (Table M4)
3416 Central America
Including individual countries (not A-Z)
3417 South America
Including individual countries (Not A-Z)
Europe
3420 General works (Table M3)
3422 Austria (Table M4)
3426 Belgium (Table M4)
3427 France (Table M4)
3429 Germany (Table M4)
3431 British Isles
Including individual countries (not A-Z)
3433 Italy (Table M4)
3435 Netherlands (Table M4)
3437 Russia. Soviet Union. Russia (Federation) (Table M4)
3442 Scandinavia
Including individual countries (not A-Z)
3447 Spain (Table M4)

History and criticism
Dance music
By region or country
Europe -- Continued
3448 Portugal (Table M4)
3449 Switzerland (Table M4)
3451.A-Z Other regions or countries, A-Z
Class here European and other regions or countries
Forms and types
3460 Ballet, pantomime, etc.
3465 Other (not A-Z)
Class here works about polka, waltz, two-step, etc.
Popular music
For works on music videos, see PN1992.8.M87
3469 Periodicals. Societies. Serials
3470 General works
By region or country
Class here general works on popular music in a particular region or country
For works about a particular kind or style of popular music, e.g., jazz, rock music, see ML3505.8+
America
Including Latin America
3475 General works
North America
3476 General works
United States
3476.8 Periodicals. Societies. Serials
3477 General works (Table M9)
Afro-American music
3478 Periodicals. Societies. Serials
3479 General works
3481 Hispanic American music
3484 Canada (Table M9)
3485 Mexico (Table M9)
3486 West Indies
3486.A1 General works
3486.A2-Z By island or country, A-Z
3487.A-Z Central and South America
3487.A1 General works
3487.A7 Argentina (Table M10)
3487.B5 Bolivia (Table M10)
3487.B7 Brazil (Table M10)
3487.C55 Chile (Table M10)
3487.C7 Colombia (Table M10)
3487.C8 Costa Rica (Table M10)
3487.E2 Ecuador (Table M10)
3487.P4 Peru (Table M10)
3487.U8 Uruguay (Table M10)
3487.V4 Venezuela (Table M10)

History and criticism
Popular music
By region or country -- Continued
Europe
3488 General works
3489 France (Table M9)
3490 Germany (Table M9)
3492 Great Britain
Including individual countries (not A-Z)
3493 Ireland (Table M9)
3494 Italy (Table M9)
3495 Netherlands (Table M9)
3496 Poland (Table M9)
3497 Russia. Soviet Union. Russia (Federation) (Table M9)
3498 Spain (Table M9)
3499.A-Z Other regions or countries, A-Z
Asia
3500 General works
3501 Japan (Table M9)
3502.A-Z Other regions or countries, A-Z
Africa
3502.9 General works
3503.A-Z By region or country, A-Z
3504 Australia (Table M9)
3505.A-Z Other regions or countries, A-Z
Types and styles
Jazz
3505.8 Periodicals. Societies. Serials
3505.9 Congresses
3506 General works
3507 Addresses, essays, lectures
By region or country
3508 United States (Table M9)
3509.A-Z Other regions or countries, A-Z
3516 Barbershop quartets. Barbershop choruses
3518 Big band music. Jazz band music. Dance band music. Dance orchestra music
Bluegrass music
3519 Periodicals. Societies. Serials
3520 General works
Blues. Rhythm and blues
Including traditional blues
3520.8 Periodicals. Societies. Serials
3521 General works
Country music
3523 Periodicals. Societies. Serials
3524 General works
3526 Disco music
3527 Doo-wop
3527.8 Funk
3528 Honky-tonk music
3528.5 House music

History and criticism
Popular music
Types and styles -- Continued
3529 New Age music
3530 Ragtime music
3531 Rap music
3532 Reggae music
Rock music
For works on rock music videos, see PN1992.8.M87
3533.8 Periodicals. Societies. Serials
3534 General works
3535 Rockabilly music
3535.5 Salsa
3536 Skiffle
3537 Soul music
3539 Swamp pop
3540 Techno music
3541 Western swing music
National music
Class here works about folk, national, ethnic, patriotic, political music, etc.
For collections of national music with critical or historical commentary, see M1627+
For popular music, see ML3469+
3544 Periodicals. Societies. Serials
3544.5 Festivals. Congresses
3545 General works
By region or country
America
3549 General works (Table M3)
Including Latin America
North America
3550 General works (Table M3)
United States
3551 General works (Table M4)
3553 British American
3554 Irish American
3555 German American. Scandinavian American. Dutch American
3556 Afro-American
Including spirituals
For Afro-American gospel music, see ML3186.8+
For blues, traditional or popular, see ML3520.8+
For general works on Afro-American popular music, see ML3478+
For types and styles of Afro-American popular music, e.g., jazz, soul music, see ML3505.8+
3557 Indian
3558 Latin American
Including Creole

History and criticism
National music
By region or country
America
North America
United States -- Continued
3560.A-Z Other ethnic groups, A-Z
3561.A-Z Special songs. By topic or title of song, A-Z
e.g.
3561.S8 Star-spangled banner
3561.W3 War songs
3562 Other topics (not A-Z)
3563 Canada (Table M4)
3565 West Indies
Including individual countries (not A-Z)
3570 Mexico (Table M4)
3572 Central America
Including individual countries (not A-Z)
South America
3575.A2 General works (Table M7)
3575.A3-Z By region or country, A-Z
Europe
3580 General works (Table M3)
3586 Austria (Table M4)
3590 Czechoslovakia. Czech Republic (Table M4)
3591 Slovakia (Table M4)
3593 Hungary (Table M4)
Balkan Peninsula
3600 General works (Table M3)
3601 Albania (Table M4)
3602 Bulgaria (Table M4)
3604 Greece (Table M4)
3608 Romania (Table M4)
3610 Yugoslavia (Table M4)
3611.A-Z Other regions and countries, A-Z
3611.B54 Bosnia and Hercegovina (Table M8)
3611.C76 Croatia (Table M8)
3611.I745 Istria (Table M8)
3611.M3 Macedonia (Republic) (Table M8)
3611.S47 Serbia (Table M8)
3611.S62 Slovenia (Table M8)
Belgium
Including Netherlands to about 1600
3615 General works (Table M4)
3616.A-Z By topic or title of song, A-Z
3617 Other topics (not A-Z)
3619 Finland (Table M4)
France
3620 General works (Table M4)
3621.A-Z By topic or title of song, A-Z
e.g.
3621.C65 Commune, 1871

History and criticism
National music
By region or country
Europe
France
Songs. By topic or title of song, A-Z -- Continued
3621.M37 Marseillaise
3621.P76 Protest songs
3621.R48 Revolution, 1789-1793
3621.W37 War songs
3622 Other topics (not A-Z)
Germany
3630 General works (Table M4)
3645.A-Z By topic or title of song, A-Z
e.g.
3645.N36 Napoleon I, Emperor of the French
3646 Other topics (not A-Z)
British Isles
3650 General works (Table M3)
3652 England (Table M4)
3653 Wales (Table M4)
3654 Ireland (Table M4)
3655 Scotland (Table M4)
3656.A-Z By topic or title of song, A-Z
e.g.
3656.G6 God save the King
3657 Other topics (not A-Z)
Italy
3660 General works (Table M4)
3661.A-Z By topic or title of song, A-Z
3662 Other topics (not A-Z)
Netherlands
For Netherlands to about 1600, see ML3615+
3670 General works (Table M4)
3671.A-Z By topic or title of song, A-Z
3672 Other topics (not A-Z)
3677 Poland (Table M4)
3680 Russia. Soviet Union. Russia (Federation) (Table M4)
For former Soviet republics in Asia, see ML3740+
3681.A-Z Baltic States
3681.A1 General works (Table M7)
3681.E8 Estonia (Table M8)
3681.L4 Latvia (Table M8)
3681.L6 Lithuania (Table M8)
3684 Belarus (Table M4)
3689 Moldova (Table M4)
3690 Ukraine (Table M4)
Scandinavia
3700 General works (Table M3)
3702 Denmark (Table M4)

ML

History and criticism
National music
By region or country
Europe
Scandinavia -- Continued
3704 Norway (Table M4)
3706 Sweden (Table M4)
3708 Other
Spain
3710 General works (Table M4)
3712 Flamenco. Cante hondo
3713.A-Z By topic or title of song, A-Z
3714 Other topics (not A-Z)
Portugal
3717 General works (Table M4)
3718.A-Z By topic or title of song, A-Z
3719 Other topics (not A-Z)
Switzerland
3720 General works (Table M4)
3721 Yodeling
3722.A-Z By topic or title of song, A-Z
e.g.
3722.N54 Nikolaus, von der Flüe, Saint, 1417-1487
3723 Other topics (not A-Z)
3730.A-Z Other European countries (not A-Z)
Asia
3740 General works (Table M3)
3742 Saudi Arabia (Table M4)
3744 Armenia (Table M4)
3746 China (Table M4)
3747 Taiwan (Table M4)
3748 India (Table M4)
3750 Japan (Table M4)
3752 Korea (Table M4)
Including South Korea
3753 Korea (North) (Table M4)
3754 Israel. Palestine (Table M4)
3756 Iran (Table M4)
3757 Turkey (Table M4)
3758.A-Z Other regions or countries, A-Z
3760 Africa (Table M3)
3770 Australia, Oceania, etc. (Table M3)
3775.A-Z Other, A-Z
3776 Music of the Jews
Class here works about secular music of the Jews in all countries
For ancient music, see ML166
For sacred vocal music, see ML3195
3780 Trade, labor, sea, hunting, etc., songs
3785 Musical criticism

3790 Music trade
For biographies of individual manufacturers of instruments, see ML424.A+
For biographies of individual music publishers, printers, dealers, see ML427.A+
For collective biographies of manufacturers of instruments, see ML404
For collective biographies of music publishers, printers, dealers, see ML405
3792 Sound recording companies
3795 Musical life
Class here works about social and economic conditions, organization, reform, statistics, etc.
Cf. ML70+, Music as a professison
Musical research
Including works on the methods of research
Musicology
3797 General works
3797.1 Addresses, essays, lectures
Ethnomusicology
3797.6 Periodicals. Societies. Serials
3797.7 Congresses
3798 General works
3799 Addresses, essays, lectures
Philosophy and physics of music
Including metaphysics and origin of music
3800 General works
Acoustics and physics
3805 General works
3807 Musical sounds
Class here works about tone, harmonics, overtones, etc.
3809 Intervals, temperament, etc.
3811 Tonality, atonality, polytonality, etc
3812 Scales
Including church modes, etc.
3813 Rhythm
3815 Harmony
3817 Other (not A-Z)
Physiology
3820 General works
Hand (Piano), see MT221
Hand (Violin), see MT261
Voice, see MT821
Psychology
3830 General works
3832 Rhythm
3834 Melody
3836 Harmony
3838 Other (not A-Z)
For moral influence of music, see ML3920
3840 Color and music
Aesthetics

ML

Philosophy and physics of music
Aesthetics -- Continued
3845 General works
3847 The beautiful in music
3849 Relations between music and other arts
Cf. ML68, Radio, television, etc., and music
Cf. ML79+, Literary authors and music
Cf. ML85, Music and musical instruments in art
For influence of music on literature, see PN56.M87
3850 Rhythm
3851 Melody
3852 Harmony
3853 Interpretation
3854 Absolute (instrumental) music
3855 Program music
Dramatic music
3857 General works
3858 Opera, ballet, opera-ballet, etc.
3860 Incidental music
3861 Melodrama
3862 Other
Sacred music
3865 General works
3867 Oratorio
3869 Church music
3871 Other (not A-Z)
Secular vocal music (non-dramatic)
3872 General works
3873 Choral music
3875 Song
Including lied, ballad, etc.
3877 Other (not A-Z)
Criticism
3880 General works
3890 The musical canon
Class here works on that group of compositions generally accepted as superior and lasting
For works on the canon as a musical form, see ML446
3915 Methodology and practice of criticism
Moral influence and therapeutic use of music
Including influence on animals
For works about music in special education, see MT17
3919 Periodicals. Societies. Serials
3920 General works
3922 Music in the workplace
3923 Music and physical education
Literature for children
Cf. MT740+, Instrumental techniques for children
For works on special subjects, see the subject, e.g., ML459-ML1380, Instruments and instrumental music
3928 General works

Literature for children -- Continued
Biography
3929 Collective
3930.A-Z Individual, A-Z
Including works on musical groups
Cutters listed below are provided as examples
3930.B39 Beatles
3930.C4 Chaĭkovskiĭ, Petr Il'ich, 1840-1893
Tchaikovsky, Peter Ilich, 1840-1893, see ML3930.C4
3930.W2 Wagner, Richard, 1813-1883

Musical instruction and study
For periodicals and serials, see ML1+
Theory and history of music education
1 General works
Including general music instruction for educational levels through high school
For music instruction in colleges and universities, see MT18
(2.5) Music study by Americans in Europe
See ML385-ML406, Collective biography, or ML410-ML429, Individual biography
3.A-Z By region or country, A-Z
Individual institutions. By city, A-Z
4.A-Z United States
Assign two Cutters, the first for the city, the second for the name of the institution
Under each institution:
.x1 *General works*
.x3 *Catalogs, calendars, etc. By date*
.x4 *History*
.x5 *Annual reports. By date*
.x6 *Special (irregular) reports*
.x7 *Programs*
.x9 *Other*
5.A-Z Other countries
Assign two Cutters, the first for the city, the second for the name of the institution
Apply table at MT4.A-Z
Music theory
Including instruction on how to analyze musical works
For dictation and ear training, see MT35
For elements and techniques of music, see MT40+
For general music instruction for educational levels through high school, see MT1
For sight-singing and solfeggio, see MT875
5.5 Early works to 1600
Including editions of such works published after 1600, and commentaries on such works
1601-
6 General works
Assign two Cutters, the first for the author, the second for the title.
7 Rudiments. Elementary works
Class rudiments combined with instruction for a specific instrument with the instrument
9 Examinations, exercises, etc.
10 Teachers' and supervisors' manuals, etc.
Including outlines of courses
15 Charts, diagrams, etc.
17 Music in special education
Class here works on music education for exceptional children, handicapped children, etc.
For works about music therapy, see ML3920

18 Music in colleges and universities
Specific systems and methods
20 Galin-Paris-Chevé
22.A-Z Jaques-Dalcroze
Literature
Collections
22.A2-A64 By Jaques-Dalcroze and others
22.A65-A69 By Jaques-Dalcroze
e.g.
Méthode Jaques-Dalcroze
22.A7-A74 Single works. By Jaques-Dalcroze
Musical compositions for use in the method
22.A75 By Jaques-Dalcroze
22.A8 By others
22.A85-Z Works about the method
23 Kodály
24 Logier
26 Orff
30 Tonic sol-fa
32 Other (not A-Z)
33 Correspondence school, etc. methods
34 Club and study group courses
Notation
35 General works
Including dictation, ear-training, music copying, and manuscript preparation
38 Notation for the blind
39 Computer production of music notation
Composition. Elements and techniques of music
For general works on music theory, see MT5.5+
40 Composition
Including the twelve-tone system
For composition of electronic or computer music, see MT56
41 Composition using mechanical devices or prescribed formulas
42 Rhythm
44 Solmization
For sight-singing, see MT870
45 Scales
Including church modes, etc.
47 Melody
49 Thorough bass
50 Harmony
For keyboard harmony, see MT224
52 Modulation
55 Counterpoint. Polyphony
56 Electronic music. Computer music
Forms and genres
58 General works
59 Canon and fugue
For general works on counterpoint, see MT55
62 Sonata

Composition. Elements and techniques of music
Forms and genres -- Continued
64.A-Z Other, A-Z
64.C48 Chaconne
64.L23 Ländler
64.M5 Minuet
64.M65 Motion picture music
64.O6 Opera
64.P6 Polonaise
64.R6 Rondo
64.S6 Song
64.S7 String quartet
64.S8 Suite
64.S9 Symphony
64.W3 Waltz
67 Popular music
Class here works about composition, writing of song texts, etc.
Including commercials
68 Improvisation. Accompaniment. Transposition
For accompaniment of liturgical music, see MT190
Instrumentation and orchestration
Orchestra
70 General works
70.5 Orchestration for special uses
Including vocal arranging
71 Separate orchestral choirs
Class here works about string sections, wind sections, etc.
73 Band
73.5 Jazz band, dance band, etc.
74 Mandolin, etc., orchestra
75 Interpretation
Including works about phrasing, dynamics, articulation, and other performance techniques
80 Embellishment
82 Memorizing
85 Conducting. Score reading and playing
87 Community music
88 Administration and instruction of vocal groups
Including music in worship services
Analysis and appreciation of musical works
Class here works consisting primarily of analysis of musical compositions
For works about the music of individual composers that are 20% or more biographical or historical in content, see ML410+
90 General works
91 Collections of music for analysis and appreciation
92 Individual composers
Class here analytical works more general than MT100, MT115, etc.

Analysis and appreciation
of musical works -- Continued
Dramatic music
Including synopses
95 Two or more composers
100.A-Z One composer. By composer, A-Z
Including pasticcios
e.g.
Wagner, Richard, 1813-1883
100.W2 General works
100.W21 Early operas
Including Der fliegende Holländer
100.W22 Tannhäuser
100.W23 Lohengrin
100.W24 Tristan und Isolde
Ring des Nibelungen
100.W25 Complete
100.W26 Rheingold
100.W27 Walküre
100.W28 Siegfried
100.W29 Götterdämmerung
100.W3 Meistersinger
100.W31 Parsifal
Oratorios, cantatas, etc.
110 Two or more composers
115.A-Z One composer. By composer, A-Z
Songs, song cycles, etc.
120 Two or more composers
121.A-Z One composer. By composer, A-Z
Orchestral music
125 Two or more composers
130.A-Z One composer. By composer, A-Z
Chamber and solo instrumental music
140 Two or more composers
145.A-Z One composer. By composer, A-Z
e.g.
Beethoven, Ludwig van, 1770-1827
145.B4 Chamber music
145.B42 Piano sonatas
145.B422 Sonatas for violin and piano
145.B425 String quartets
146 Popular music
Class here general works and works about individual types
150 Audio-visual aids
155 Harmony, composition, etc., for children
165 Tuning
Class here general works and works on particular instruments or groups of instruments
Instrumental techniques
Cf. MT740+, Instrumental techniques for children
170 General works
172 Methods for several instruments in one work

Instrumental techniques -- Continued
Keyboard instruments
179 General works
Organ
180 General works
182 Systems and methods
Studies and exercises
For guidelines on classifying studies and exercises for solo instrument, see Studies and exercises in the Glossary and General Guidelines following the Introduction
185 General works
Special techniques
187 Pedal
189 Registration
190 Accompaniment of Gregorian chant and other liturgical music
191.A-Z Other, A-Z
191.A3 Accompaniment
191.A8 Arranging
191.C5 Chorales
191.H4 Harmony
191.I5 Improvisation
191.M6 Modulation
191.T7 Trio playing
192 Electronic keyboard instruments (Table M5)
Including synthesizers with keyboards
193 Teaching pieces
For a definition of teaching piece, see the Glossary and General Guidelines following the Introduction
Instructive editions
For a definition of instructive edition, see the Glossary and General Guidelines following the Introduction
195 Two or more composers
197 One composer
198 Self-instructors
Reed organ
200 General works
202 Systems and methods
205 Studies and exercises
208 Self-instructors
Piano
220 General works
221 Physiology of the hand
Including hand exercises
222 Systems and methods
224 Rudiments of music
Class here rudiments of music combined with piano instruction
Studies and exercises
225 General works

Instrumental techniques
Keyboard instruments
Piano
Studies and exercises -- Continued
Special techniques
226 Left hand
227 Pedal
228 Touch
Class here works about legato, staccato, melody, etc., playing
229 Wrist
Class here works about octave, chord, etc., playing
230 Thirds, sixths, etc.
231 Scales and arpeggios
232 Fingering
233 Rhythm
235 Phrasing
236 Sight reading, transposition, accompaniment, etc.
238 Polyphonic playing
239 Performance of popular music
Class here works about vamping, ragtime, vaudeville piano playing, jazz, boogie-woogie, improvisation, playing by ear, etc.
Including accompaniment
240.A-Z Other techniques, A-Z
242 Four-hand, two-piano, etc. playing
243 Teaching pieces
Instructive editions
245 Two or more composers
247 One composer
248 Self-instructors
Special kinds of piano
Including early instruments
250 General works
252 Harpsichord, etc.
255 Janko keyboard
257.A-Z Other keyboard instruments, A-Z
258 Virgil clavier, technicon, and similar instruments for practicing
Stringed instruments
259 General works
Violin
260 General works
261 Physiology of the hand
For hand exercises, see MT221
262 Systems and methods
Studies and exercises
265 General works
266 Orchestral studies
Special techniques

Instrumental techniques
Stringed instruments
Violin
Studies and exercises
Special techniques -- Continued
267 Bowing
268 Positions
269 Chords
270 Harmonics
271 Other (not A-Z)
272 Two violins
274 Teaching pieces
Instructive editions
275 Two or more composers
276 One composer
278 Self-instructors
Special styles
279.5 Fiddling. Folk-style violin playing
279.7 Jazz
Viola
280 General works
282 Systems and methods
Studies and exercises
285 General works
286 Orchestral studies
Special techniques
287 Bowing
288 Positions
289 Chords
290 Harmonics
291 Other (not A-Z)
292 Two violas
294 Teaching pieces
Instructive editions
295 Two or more composers
297 One composer
298 Self-instructors
Violoncello
300 General works
302 Systems and methods
Studies and exercises
305 General works
306 Orchestral studies
Special techniques
307 Bowing
308 Positions
309 Chords
310 Other (not A-Z)
312 Two violoncellos
314 Teaching pieces
Instructive editions
315 Two or more composers
317 One composer

Instrumental techniques
Stringed instruments
Violoncello -- Continued
318 Self-instructors
Double bass
320 General works
322 Systems and methods
330 Studies and exercises
331 Orchestral studies
333 Teaching pieces
333.4 Instructive editions
333.6 Two double basses
334 Self-instructors
335.A-Z Other stringed instruments, A-Z
335.C36 Campanula
335.C5 Ching hu
335.C56 Chui ch'in
335.C58 Chung hu
335.E7 Erh hu
335.G8 Gŭdulka
335.H36 Haegŭm
335.H4 Hardanger fiddle
335.H83 Hu hu
335.J68 Jouhikko
335.K32 Kao hu
335.M67 Morin khuur
335.P3 Pan hu
335.S7 Sǫ ū
335.T3 Ta t'ung
Early stringed instruments
336 Viola d'amore
337 Viola da gamba
338 Other
Wind instruments
339 General works
339.5 Woodwind instruments (General)
Flute
340 General works
342 Systems and methods
343 Teaching pieces
344 Instructive editions
345 Studies and exercises
346 Orchestral studies
347 Two flutes
348 Self-instructors
Other instruments of the flute family
Recorder
350 General works
351 Systems and methods
352 Studies and exercises
352.5 Teaching pieces
352.6 Instructive editions
352.7 Two recorders

Instrumental techniques
Wind instruments
Flute
Other instruments of the flute family
Recorder -- Continued
353 Self-instructors
356 Fife
For fife and drum, see MT735
357 Piccolo (Table M5)
358.A-Z Other, A-Z
358.A8 Atenteben
358.B36 Bānsurī
(358.C68) Courting flute
See MT358.N38
358.C9 Czakan
358.G3 Galoubet
358.H7 Hsiao
358.M4 Melody flute
358.N38 Native American flute
358.N4 Nāy
Ocarina, see MT526
358.O7 Orkon
358.P45 Penny whistle
358.P5 Piccolet
358.P6 Pipe
358.Q4 Quena
358.S4 Saxoflute
358.S52 Shakuhachi
358.S55 Shinobue
358.S6 Siku
358.S9 Suifūkin
358.T3 Tanso
358.T5 Ti tzu
358.T6 Tonette
359 Flageolet
Oboe
360 General works
362 Systems and methods
363 Teaching pieces
364 Instructive editions
365 Studies and exercises
366 Orchestral studies
367 Two oboes
368 Self-instructors
Other instruments of the oboe family
372 Oboette
373 Musette
374 P'iri
376 English horn
377 So na
378 Rgya-gling
379.A-Z Other, A-Z
379.N35 Nāgasvaram

Instrumental techniques
Wind instruments
Oboe
Other instruments of the oboe family
Other, A-Z -- Continued
379.T34 T‘aep‘yŏngso
Clarinet
Including A, B♭ , C, E♭ , etc.
380 General works
382 Systems and methods
383 Teaching pieces
384 Instructive editions
385 Studies and exercises
386 Orchestral studies
387 Two clarinets
388 Self-instructors
Other instruments of the clarinet family
392 Bass clarinet (Table M5)
Bassoon
400 General works
402 Systems and methods
403 Teaching pieces
404 Instructive editions
405 Studies and exercises
406 Orchestral studies
407 Two bassoons
408 Self-instructors
Other instruments of the bassoon family
412 Contrabassoon
415 Sarrusophone
418 Brass instruments (General)
Horn
420 General works
422 Systems and methods
423 Teaching pieces
424 Instructive editions
425 Studies and exercises
426 Orchestral studies
427 Two horns
428 Self-instructors
Other instruments of the horn family
432 Alphorn
Trumpet. Cornet
440 General works
442 Systems and methods
443 Teaching pieces
444 Instructive editions
445 Studies and exercises
446 Orchestral studies
447 Two instruments
448 Self-instructors
Other instruments of the trumpet family
452 Bugle

Instrumental techniques
Wind instruments
Trumpet. Cornet
Other instruments
of the trumpet family -- Continued
456 Post horn
Trombone
Including soprano, alto, tenor trombone
460 General works
462 Systems and methods
463 Teaching pieces
464 Instructive editions
465 Studies and exercises
466 Orchestral studies
467 Two trombones
468 Self-instructors
472 Bass trombone. Contrabass trombone (Table M5)
Tuba. Bass tuba. Bombardon
480 General works
482 Systems and methods
483 Teaching pieces
484 Instructive editions
485 Studies and exercises
486 Orchestral studies
487 Two instruments
488 Self-instructors
Other instruments of the bugle (saxhorn, flügelhorn) family
492 Saxhorn (Soprano)
493 Flügelhorn
494 Alto horn
495 Tenor horn
496 Baritone. Euphonium (Table M5)
497 Contrabass tuba, helicon, etc.
Saxophone
500 General works
502 Systems and methods
503 Teaching pieces
504 Instructive editions
505 Studies and exercises
506 Orchestral studies
507 Two saxophones
508 Self-instructors
510 Other instruments of the saxophone family
520 Ophicleide, serpent, and other early instruments
526 Ocarina
530 Bagpipe and similar instruments
533.A-Z Other wind instruments, A-Z
533.D53 Didjeridu
533.K36 Kazoo
533.M4 Melodica
533.S95 Syrinx
Plucked instruments

Instrumental techniques
Plucked instruments -- Continued
539 General works
Harp
540 General works
542 Systems and methods
543 Teaching pieces
544 Instructive editions
545 Studies and exercises
546 Orchestral studies
547 Two harps
548 Self-instructors
Other instruments of the harp family
552 Celtic harp
557 Piano harp and similar instruments
Banjo
560 General works
562 Systems and methods
563 Teaching pieces
564 Rudiments of music
Class here rudiments of music combined with banjo instruction
565 Studies and exercises
567 Two banjos
568 Self-instructors
569 Instructive editions
570 Other instruments of the banjo family (not A-Z)
Guitar
580 General works
582 Systems and methods
583 Teaching pieces
584 Rudiments of music
Class here rudiments of music combined with guitar instruction
585 Studies and exercises
586 Orchestral studies
587 Two guitars
588 Self-instructors
589 Instructive editions
Other instruments of the guitar family
590 Hawaiian guitar (Table M5)
592 Bandurria (Table M5)
594 Bandolon
599.A-Z Other, A-Z
599.B4 Bass guitar
599.C45 Charango
(599.C52) Cittern
See MT654.C58
599.D6 Dobro
Electric bass guitar, see MT599.B4
599.E4 Electric guitar
599.G85 Guitarrón
Mandolin

Instrumental techniques
Plucked instruments
Mandolin -- Continued
600 General works
602 Systems and methods
603 Teaching pieces
604 Rudiments of music
Class here rudiments of music combined with mandolin instruction
605 Studies and exercises
606 Orchestral studies
607 Two mandolins
608 Self-instructors
608.5 Instructive editions
Other instruments of the mandolin family
610 General works
611 Mandola
612 Mandoloncello
Zither
620 General works
622 Systems and methods
623 Teaching pieces
624 Rudiments of music
Class here rudiments of music combined with zither instruction
625 Studies and exercises
627 Two zithers
628 Self-instructors
628.5 Instructive editions
Other instruments of the zither family
632 Autoharp (Table M5)
634.A-Z Other, A-Z
634.A85 Audeharp
634.B84 Bulbultarang
634.C4 Cither harp
634.G5 Guitar zither
634.H36 Harp-lute guitar
634.H37 Harp zither
634.H38 Harpola
634.I3 Ideal harp
634.K3 Kannel
634.K35 Kantele
634.K65 Kokle
634.M35 Mandolin guitar
634.M44 Meloharp
634.M48 Meta-harp
634.N3 New century cither
634.N48 New century harp
634.O58 Ongnyugŭm
634.P5 Piano-zither
634.V35 Valiha
634.Y36 Yanggŭm
634.Z58 Zitho-harp

Instrumental techniques
Plucked instruments -- Continued
640 Lute (Table M5)
643 Balalaika, dömbra, etc. (Table M5)
644 Lyre
645 Ukulele (Table M5)
646 Banjulele
647 Tambi
648 Cuatro
649 Sitar (Table M5)
650 Tambura
654.A-Z Other, A-Z
654.A7 Appalachian dulcimer
654.B3 Bağlama
654.B35 Bandura
654.B69 Bouzouki
654.C47 Cheng
654.C5 Ch'in
654.C58 Cittern
654.E6 Epinette des Vosges
654.K4 Kayagŭm
654.K7 Koto
654.L58 Liu ch'in
654.M38 Mbira
654.O9 Oud
654.P5 P'i p'a
654.S26 San hsien
654.S5 Shamisen
654.S58 Shudraga
654.V56 Vina
654.Y83 Yüeh ch'in
Percussion and other instruments
655 General works (Table M5)
660 Timpani (Table M5)
662 Drum, bass drum, snare drum, etc. (Table M5)
Including drum set and instruction for the entire batterie
663 Bongo. Conga drums (Table M5)
664 Tabla (Table M5)
670 Glass harmonica
680 Accordion (Piano accordion) (Table M5)
681 Concertina. Button-key accordion (Table M5)
Mouth organs
682 Harmonica (Table M5)
683 Kaen
684 Sheng
685 Shō
700 Player-piano and similar instruments
(705) Whistling
See MT949.5
710 Carillon, bell ringing, etc.
Including change ringing, peals, etc.

Instrumental techniques
Percussion and other instruments -- Continued
711 Handbell ringing
Including change ringing for handbells
717 Dulcimer (Table M5)
719 Xylophone and similar instruments (Table M5)
Including marimba, vibraphone, etc.
720 Tubular bells. Chimes
722 Implements put to musical use
Class here works about saws, kitchen utensils, etc.
723 Computer sound processing
Class here works on the production and manipulation of music by digital techniques
724 Electronic instruments (not A-Z)
Class here works on analog electronic musical instruments, including Ondes Martenot, Theremin, and Trautonium
For works on composing computer music, see MT56
For works on electronic keyboard instruments, including synthesizers with keyboards, see MT192
724.5 Electronic percussion instruments. Drum machines
725.A-Z Other, A-Z
725.B3 Balo
725.B55 Bodhrán
725.B6 Bones
725.C4 Castanets
725.C45 Changgo
725.C5 Chin ch'ien pan
725.C55 Cimbalom
725.C6 Claves
725.C9 Cymbals
725.D37 Darabukka
725.G4 Gender
725.G53 Ghatam
725.G8 Guṃlā
725.H37 Hardwood drum
725.H87 Hurdy-gurdy
725.J5 Jew's harp
725.L6 Lo ku
725.M4 Maracas
725.M7 Mridanga
725.P5 Phonofiddle
Piano, Toy, see MT725.T7
725.P8 Pung
725.S7 Steel drum
725.T3 Tambourine
725.T38 Tavil
725.T5 Tinglik
725.T7 Toy piano
725.T8 Tubaphone. Tubuphone
725.Y3 Yang ch'in

Instrumental techniques
Percussion and other instruments
Other, A-Z -- Continued
725.Y34 Yanggŭm
725.Y66 Yoochin (Dulcimer)
Ensembles
Chamber music
728 General works
Instructive editions
728.2 Two or more composers
728.3 One composer
730 Orchestra
Band
733 General works
733.4 Marching bands and maneuvers
733.5 Drum majoring
733.6 Baton twirling
733.7 Big band. Dance band. Jazz band
734 Mandolin, etc., orchestra
735 Field music
Class here works about signals and fife and drum music
737 Motion picture accompanying
Instrumental techniques for children
Cf. MT937, School music instrumental methods
740 General works
742 Systems and methods (General)
Piano
745 General works
746 Systems and methods
750 Special techniques
755 Studies and exercises
756 Four hands. Two pianos
758 Teaching pieces
Violin. Viola
760 General works
761 Systems and methods
765 Special techniques
775 Studies and exercises
776 Two violins
778 Teaching pieces
Violoncello
785 General works
786 Systems and methods
790 Special techniques
795 Studies and exercises
796 Two violoncellos
798 Teaching pieces
Other instruments
800 General works
801.A-Z By instrument, A-Z
801.A3 Accordion
801.A66 Appalachian dulcimer

Instrumental techniques
Instrumental techniques for children
Other instruments
By instrument, A-Z -- Continued

801.A85 Autoharp
801.B3 Banjo
801.B5 Bells
801.B72 Brass instruments (General)
801.C6 Clarinet
801.C66 Cornet
801.C8 Cuatro
801.D65 Double bass
801.D7 Drum
801.F4 Flageolet
801.F5 Flute
Flutophone, see MT801.T6
801.G8 Guitar
801.H35 Handbells
801.H4 Harmonica
801.H7 Horn
801.M3 Mandolin
Melody flute, see MT801.T6
801.O7 Organ
801.P46 Penny whistle
801.P55 Pipe
801.R4 Recorder
801.S4 Saxophone
801.S5 Sheng
801.S8 Stringed instruments (General)
801.T6 Tonette, flutophone, melody flute, and similar melody instruments
801.T67 Trombone
801.T7 Trumpet
801.T8 Tuba
801.U4 Ukulele
801.W5 Wind instruments (General)
801.X9 Xylophone and similar instruments
810 Ensembles
Class here orchestral music, chamber music, rhythm band, etc.

Singing and vocal technique
820 General works
821 Physiology and care of the voice
Cf. RF511.S55, Voice disorders of singers
823 History of vocal instruction and study
Systems and methods
825 American
830 English
835 French
840 German
845 Italian
850 Other (not A-Z)

Singing and vocal technique -- Continued
853 Systems using audio-visual aids
Cf. MT150, Audio-visual aids
Special techniques
855 General works
860 Chanting (plain, Gregorian, etc.)
Including intonations, etc.
870 Sight-singing
Including solfeggio
875 Chorus and part-singing
878 Breathing
882 Tone production
883 Pronunciation. Diction
885 Studies and exercises
890 Instructive editions. Teaching pieces
892 Interpretation, phrasing, expression, etc.
893 Self-instructors
Vocal techniques for children
898 General works
900 Systems and methods
905 Special techniques
915 Choir training
School music
918 General works
Kindergarten
920 General works
925 Methods and exercises
Elementary schools. Junior high schools. High schools
930 General works
935 Vocal methods
937 Instrumental methods
Cf. MT740+, Instrumental techniques for children
945 Studies and exercises
948 Action songs. Drill songs. Musical games
Cf. M1993, Action songs. Drill songs. Musical games
949.5 Whistling
950 Music to accompany instruction in ballet, gymnastics, rhythmic movement, etc.
Cf. GV1755+, Folk dance instruction
Musical theater
Class here works about opera, musicals, etc.
955 Production
Class here works about direction, costume, scenery, etc.
956 Performing
Class here works on singing, acting, etc.
960 Music in theaters

Assign Cutters for regions as needed in individual classes

.A3 Alabama
.A4 Alaska
.A5 Arizona
.A7 Arkansas
.C15 California
.C3 Carolina (General)
.C5 Colorado
.C7 Connecticut
.D3 Dakota (General)
.D33 Delaware
.D5 District of Columbia
.F6 Florida
.G4 Georgia
.H4 Hawaii
.I2 Idaho
.I3 Illinois
.I39 Indiana
.I6 Iowa
.K2 Kansas
.K4 Kentucky
.L8 Louisiana
.M2 Maine
.M3 Maryland
.M4 Massachusetts
.M5 Michigan
.M55 Minnesota
.M6 Mississippi
.M68 Missouri
.M7 Montana
.N36 Nebraska
.N5 Nevada
.N53 New Hampshire
.N55 New Jersey
.N57 New Mexico
.N6 New York
.N85 North Carolina
.N88 North Dakota
.O37 Ohio
.O5 Oklahoma
.O66 Oregon
.P4 Pennsylvania
.R47 Rhode Island
.S6 South Carolina
.S8 South Dakota
.T3 Tennessee
.T35 Texas
.U89 Utah
.V5 Vermont
.V8 Virginia
.W3 Washington
Washington (D.C.), see .D5

TABLES

.W5	West Virginia
.W6	Wisconsin
.W9	Wyoming

Assign the five numbers in the span as follows:

1 Miscellaneous collections

Original compositions

2 Collections

3 Separate works

Arrangements

4 Collections

5 Separate works

(1 NO.)

Under each region, add to the class number as follows:

0	General works
0.1	Addresses, essays, lectures
	By period
0.2	Early to 1700
0.3	1701-1800
0.4	1801-1900
0.5	1901-2000

Under each country, add to the class number as follows:

0	General works
0.1	Addresses, essays, lectures
	By period
0.2	Early to 1700
0.3	1701-1800
0.4	1801-1900
0.5	1901-2000
0.7A-Z	By state, province, etc., A-Z For regions and states of the United States, see Table M1
0.8A-Z	By city, A-Z For works on a specific city in relation to a topic, see the topic, e.g., ML1711.8.P5, Opera in Philadelphia; for works on a specific society, including performing ensembles, see ML26-ML28; for works on a specific festival, including performance festivals, see ML36-ML38
0.9	Other

TABLE OF SUBDIVISIONS FOR INSTRUMENTAL INSTRUCTION AND STUDY

Add to the class number as follows:

0	General works
0.2	Systems and methods
0.3	Studies and exercises
0.4	Orchestral studies
0.5	Teaching pieces
0.6	Instructive editions
0.7	Two instruments
0.8	Self-instructors

By language, A-Z
Use an initial letter for the language according to English terminology, e.g., .E1-.E99 English, .G1-.G99 German, etc. If more than one language is present, one of which is Latin, assign .L
For special texts not listed below see the medium of performance, e.g., M2072, for Domine probasti me (Psalm 139) for mixed chorus with keyboard accompaniment

.x1	Two or more of the texts listed below For combinations like Magnificat and Nunc dimittis, etc., see under particular headings
.x11	Adeste fidelis
.x114	Adoro te
.x12	Agnus Dei (O Lamb of God)
.x13	Alma Redemptoris Mater
.x14	Amens
.x144	Antiphons Class here sets only For individual antiphons, see M6 .x13, etc.
.x15	Asperges me
.x16	Ave Maria
.x161	Ave Maris Stella
.x163	Ave Regina laetare
.x165	Ave verum corpus
.x168	Beatitudes
.x169	Beatus vir, qui non abiit; Psalm 1
.x17	Benedic anima mea et omnia (Bless the Lord, O my soul); Psalm 103
.x18	Benedicite omnia opera (O all ye works of the Lord)
.x2	Benedictus Dominus (Blessed be the Lord); Psalm 144
.x21	Benedictus qui venit (Blessed is He that cometh)
	Bless the Lord, O my soul, see .x17
	Blessed be the Lord, see .x2
	Blessed is He that cometh, see .x21
.x22	Bone pastor
.x23	Bonum est confiteri (It is a good thing); Psalm 92
.x25	Cantate Domino canticum novum, cantate Domino (O sing unto the Lord); Psalm 96
.x27	Collects Class here sets only
.x28	Cor Jesu
	Creeds
.x3	Nicene: Credo in unum Deum (I believe in one God, the Father almighty)
.x31	Athanasian
.x32	Apostles
.x34	De profundis; Psalm 130
.x35	Deus misereatur (God be merciful); Psalm 67
.x37	Dies irae
.x373	Dixit Dominus; Psalm 110
.x38	Ecce panis
.x382	Ecce sacerdos

TABLES

.x39 Gaude Virgo
.x4 Gloria in excelsis Deo (Glory be to the Lord on high)
.x41 Gloria Patri (Glory be to the Father)
.x413 Gloria tibi (Glory be to thee)
Glory be to the Father, see .x41
Glory be to the Lord on high, see .x4
Glory be to thee, see .x413
God be merciful, see .x35
.x416 Graduals
  Class here sets only
  Including works with offertories added
  For separate sets of offertories, see .x73
.x42 Haec dies
Have mercy upon me, O God, see .x62
Holy, Holy, Holy, Lord God of hosts, see .x8
.x43 Hymns
  Class here sets only
I believe in one God, the Father almighty, see .x3
.x435 In te, Domine, speravi (In thee, O Lord, do I put my trust); Psalm 31
In thee, O Lord, do I put my trust, see .x435
.x438 Introits
  Class here sets only
It is a good thing, see .x23
.x44 Jesu dulcis memoria
.x445 Jesu Redemptor omnium
.x45 Jubilate Deo omnis terra, servite Domino; Psalm 100
.x47 Justus ut palma
.x5 Kyrie eleison (Lord have mercy upon us)
  For the Greek text, Kyrie eleison, assign the Cutter .L
.x52 Lauda Sion
.x53 Laudate Dominum in sanctis eius; Psalm 150
.x535 Laudate, pueri, Dominum; Psalm 113
.x54 Libera me
Lift up your hearts, see .x85
.x55 Litanies
  Class here sets only
Lord have mercy upon us, see .x5
Lord now lettest Thou, see .x7
Lord's prayer, see .x74
.x59 Lucis creator
.x6 Magnificat (My soul doth magnify)
  Class here Magnificats with or without Nunc dimittis following
.x61 Media vita
.x62 Miserere mei, Deus, secundum magnum misericordiam (Have mercy upon me, O God); Psalm 51
My soul doth magnify, see .x6
.x67 Nato nobis Salvatore
.x7 Nunc dimittis (Lord now lettest Thou)
  Class here separate works only
  Cf. .x6, Magnificat

	O all ye works of the Lord, see .x18
	O come let us sing, see .x95
.x713	O cor amoris victima
	O Lamb of God, see .x12
.x718	O sacrum convivium
.x72	O salutaris (hostia)
	O sing unto the Lord, see .x25
.x73	Offertories
	Class here sets only
.x735	Pange lingua
.x737	Panis angelicus
.x74	Pater noster (Lord's prayer)
.x745	Pie Jesu
.x75	Processionals
	Class here sets only
	Psalm 1, see .x169
	Psalm 31, see .x435
	Psalm 51, see .x62
	Psalm 67, see .x35
	Psalm 92, see .x23
	Psalm 95, see .x95
	Psalm 96, see .x25
	Psalm 100, see .x45
	Psalm 103, see .x17
	Psalm 110, see .x373
	Psalm 113, see .x535
	Psalm 130, see .x34
	Psalm 144, see .x2
	Psalm 150, see .x53
.x756	Quid retribuam
.x76	Recessionals
	Class here sets only
.x77	Regina Caeli
.x78	Responses
	Class here sets only
	Sadly stood the Mother weeping, see .x82
.x79	Salve Regina
.x8	Sanctus (Holy, Holy, Holy, Lord God of hosts)
.x82	Stabat Mater dolorosa (Sadly stood the Mother weeping)
.x85	Sursum corda (Lift up your hearts)
.x87	Tantum ergo
.x9	Te Deum laudamus (We praise Thee O God)
.x91	Terra tremuit
.x914	Tollite hostias
.x916	Tota pulchra
.x918	Tu es Petrus
.x92	Veni Creator Spiritus
.x94	Veni Sancte Spiritus
.x95	Venite, exultemus Domino (O come let us sing); Psalm 95
.x96	Vesper prayers, hymns, etc.
	Class here sets only
	For vesper services see M2014.6, Catholic, and M2016.4, Anglican

TABLES

.x97	Vidi aquam
.x975	Virgin Mary Class here sets not elsewhere provided for, as e.g., under Litanies
	We praise Thee O God, see .x9

Under each region, add to the class number as follows:

.x	General works
.x1	Addresses, essays, lectures
	By period
.x2	Early to 1700
.x3	1701-1800
.x4	1801-1900
.x5	1901-2000

Under each country, add to the class number as follows:

.x	General works
.x1	Addresses, essays, lectures
	By period
.x2	Early to 1700
.x3	1701-1800
.x4	1801-1900
.x5	1901-2000
.x7A-Z	By state, province, etc., A-Z For regions and states of the United States, see Table M1
.x8A-Z	By city, A-Z For works on a specific city in relation to a topic, see the topic, e.g., ML1711.8.P5, Opera in Philadelphia; for works on a specific society, including performing ensembles, see ML26-ML28; for works on a specific festival, including performance festivals, see ML36-ML38
.x9	Other

Under each country, add to the class number as follows:

0.1 Addresses, essays, lectures

0.7A-Z By state, province, etc., A-Z

For regions and states of the United States, see Table M1

0.8A-Z By city, A-Z

Under each country, add to the class number as follows:

.x1 Addresses, essays, lectures

.x7A-Z By state, province, etc.

For regions and states of the United States, see Table M1

.x8A-Z By city, A-Z

A

Aaronic Order
  Hymns: M2131.A15
Abolitionists
  Vocal music: M1664.A35, M1665.A35
Absolute music
  Philosophy and aesthetics: ML3854
Accompaniment
  Instruction and study: MT190, MT236, MT737, MT950
Accordion: ML1083
  Bibliography: ML128.A3
  Dictionaries: ML102.A2
  Instruction and study: MT680
    For children: MT801.A3
Accordion and piano music: M284.A3, M285.A3
Accordion band music: M1362
Accordion music: M175.A4
  Concertos: M1039.4.A3, M1139.4.A3
  Duets (trios, etc.): M1362
  For children: M1385.A4
Acoustics and physics: ML3805+
Acting in musical theater: MT956
Action songs: MT948
Advent music
  Choruses, etc., Unaccompanied: M2088.A4, M2098.A4
  Choruses, etc., with keyboard: M2068.A4, M2078.A4
  For children: M2191.A4
  Liturgy and ritual: M2148.3.A31+
  Organ: M14.4.A4, M14.5.A4
  Songs: M2114.8.A4
Advertising flyers: ML45
Aeronautics
  Vocal music: M1977.A4, M1978.A4
Aesthetics: ML3845+
Africa
  History and criticism: ML350, ML3502.5+, ML3760
  Instruments: ML544
  Vocal music: M1830+
Afro-American folk music
  History and criticism: ML3556
Afro-American music
  History and criticism: ML3478+
Afro-Americans
  Music
    Bibliography: ML128.B45
  Vocal music: M1670+
Aged
  Vocal music: M1977.S45, M1978.S45
Albania
  History and criticism: ML3601
  Vocal music: M1724+
Alboka: ML990.A5
Alcoholics Anonymous
  Vocal music: M1920.A35, M1921.A35
Algeria
  Vocal music: M1838.A4+
Alhambra, Order of
  Vocal music: M1905.A46, M1906.A46
All Saints Day music
  Choruses, etc., Unaccompanied: M2088.A5, M2098.A5
  Choruses, etc., with keyboard: M2068.A5, M2078.A5
  Songs: M2114.8.A5
Alleluia (Music)
  Bibliography: ML128.A45
Almanacs: ML12+
Alphorn
  Instruction and study: MT432
Alphorn music: M110.A47
Alto flute and piano music: M240+
Alto flute music: M60+
  Concertos: M1020+, M1120+
Alto horn
  Instruction and study: MT494
Alto horn and piano music: M270.A4, M271.A4
Amaranth, Order of
  Vocal music: M1905.A55, M1906.A55
Ambrosian rite: M2154.6.A45
America (Song): M1630.3.A5
America the beautiful: M1630.3.A6
American Federation of Labor
  Vocal music: M1664.L3, M1665.L3
American Gold Star Mothers, Inc.
  Vocal music: M1676.G6
American Independent Party
  Vocal music: M1664.A55, M1665.A55
American Legion
  Ladies Auxiliary
    Vocal music: M1676.A5+
  Vocal music: M1676.A5+

American Party
Vocal music: M1664.K5, M1665.K5
American Revolution
Bicentennial, 1776-1976
Vocal music: M1677.4
American Revolution, 1775-1783
Vocal music: M1631
American sheet music: M1.A1+, M20.C58+
Amish
Hymns: M2131.A4
Anabaptists
Hymns: M2131.A45
Anacreontic song: M1630.3.S68
Analysis, appreciation: MT90+
Bibliography: ML128.A7
Ancient Arabic Order of the Nobles of the Mystic Shrine for North America
Vocal music: M1900.M4, M1901.M4
Ancient Egyptian Order of Scioto
Vocal music: M1900.M42, M1901.M42
Anecdotes: ML65
Anglican church music
History and criticism: ML3166
Anglican Church of Canada
Liturgy and ritual: M2171.C3
Anglican Communion: M2016+
Instruction and study: M2168.7
Liturgy and ritual: M2167+
Animals
Vocal music: M1977.A6, M1978.A6
Animals and music: ML3919+
Anthems
For children: M2190+
Antiphonaries (Music): M2149.A+
Antiquarian booksellers
Catalogs: ML152
Antiques
Vocal music: M1977.A65, M1978.A65
Antislavery movements
Vocal music: M1664.A35, M1665.A35
Apollo harp music: M175.A5
Apostolic Christian Church
Hymns: M2131.A5
Appalachian dulcimer: ML1015.A6
Bibliography: ML128.A67
Instruction and study: MT654.A7
For children: MT801.A66
Appalachian dulcimer music: M142.A7
Arab countries
History and criticism: ML189, ML34
Vocal music: M1828
Arará: ML1038.A7
Archery
Vocal music: M1977.S705, M1978.S7
Archlute music: M142.A8
Argentina
History and criticism: ML231, ML3487.A7
Instruments: ML486.A7
Vocal music: M1687.A7, M1688.A7
Arias: M1611+
Armenia
History and criticism: ML334, ML3744
Vocal music: M1800+
Armenian rite: M2154.6.A76
Art: ML89
Catalogs: ML140
Artists
Vocal music: M1977.A7, M1978.A7
Arts and music: ML3849
Ascension Day music
Choruses, etc., Unaccompanied: M2088.A6, M2098.A6
Choruses, etc., with keyboard: M2068.A6, M2078.A6
Liturgy and ritual: M2149.5.V52
Songs: M2114.8.A6
Asia
History and criticism: ML330+, ML3500+, ML3740+
Instruments: ML525+
Vocal music: M1795+
Associations, institutions, etc.: ML25+, ML32+
Atabaque: ML1038.A8
Atenteben
Instruction and study: MT358.A8
Atoms
Vocal music: M1977.A8, M1978.A8
Atonality
Bibliography: ML128.T9
History: ML3811
Audeharp
Instruction and study: MT634.A85
Audio-visual aids: MT150
Augustinian rite: M2154.4.A9

Australia
History and criticism: ML360, ML3504, ML3770
Instruments: ML547
Vocal music: M1840+
Austria
History and criticism: ML246, ML3586
Instruments: ML491
Vocal music: M1702+
Autoharp: ML1015.A9
Instruction and study: MT632
For children: MT801.A85
Autoharp music: M175.A8
For children: M1385.A8
Automobile racing
Vocal music: M1977.S707, M1978.S707
Autumn
Vocal music: M1977.S413, M1978.S413
Aviation
Vocal music: M1977.A4, M1978.A4
Awards: ML75.5+
Bibliography: ML128.P68
Azerbaijan
Vocal music: M1824.A9+, M1825.A98+

B

Bağlama: ML1015.B23
Instruction and study: MT654.B3
Bagpipe: ML980
Bibliography: ML128.B17
Instruction and study: MT530
Bagpipe and piano music: M270.B3, M271.B3
Bagpipe music: M145
Bahais
Hymns: M2145.B34
Balalaika: ML1015.B24
Instruction and study: MT643
Balalaika and piano music: M282.B3, M283.B3
Balalaika music: M142.B2
Concertos: M1037.4.B3
Balkan Peninsula
History and criticism: ML250+, ML3600+
Vocal music: M1712+
Ballad operas
Librettos: ML50.7
Ballets: M1520+
Bibliography: ML128.B2
History and criticism: ML3460
Librettos: ML51+
Philosophy and aesthetics: ML3858
Stories, plots, etc.: MT95+
Balloons
Vocal music: M1977.B3, M1978.B3
Balo
Instruction and study: MT725.B3
Baltic States
History and criticism: ML302+, ML3681.A+
Instruments: ML508.A+
Bambuso sonoro music: M175.B17
Band music: M1200+
Bibliography: ML128.B23
Graded lists: ML132.B3
Discography: ML156.4.B3
For children: M1420
History and criticism: ML1299+, ML3518
Performance: MT733+
Band music, Arranged: M1254+
Bandolon
Instruction and study: MT594
Bandonion: ML1083
Bandonion and piano music: M284.B33, M285.B33
Bandonion music: M175.B2
Concertos: M1039.4.B3, M1139.4.B3
For children: M1385.B34
Bandora
Bibliography: ML128.B235
Bands
Dictionaries: ML102.B35
Bandura: ML1015.B25
Instruction and study: MT654.B35
Bandurria: ML1015.B26
Instruction and study: MT592
Bandurria music: M142.B3
Banjo: ML1015.B3
Instruction and study: MT560+
For children: MT801.B3
Banjo and piano music: M274+
Banjo music: M120+, MT563, MT569
Discography: ML156.4.B36
For children: M1385.B35
Banjulele
Instruction and study: MT646

Big band music
  Bibliography: ML128.B29
  Discography: ML156.4.B5
  History and criticism: ML3518
  Performance: MT733.7
Big bands
  Dictionaries: ML102.B5
Biography: ML385+
Biological diversity conservation
  Vocal music: M1977.C53, M1978.C53
Birbynė music: M110.B57
Birds
  Vocal music: M1977.B5, M1978.B5
Birthdays
  Vocal music: M1977.B53, M1978.B53
Biwa: ML1015.B55
Biwa music: M142.B5
Blind, Music for the
  Bibliography: ML128.B47
Blue Lodge
  Vocal music: M1900.M31, M1901.M31
Blue Star Mothers
  Vocal music: M1676.B5
Bluegrass music
  Discography: ML156.4.C7
  History and criticism: ML3519+
Blues (Music)
  Bibliography: ML128.B49
  Dictionaries: ML102.B6
  Discography: ML156.4.B6
  History and criticism: ML3520.8+
B'nai B'rith
  Vocal music: M1905.B5, M1906.B5
Bodhrán: ML1038.B63
  Instruction and study: MT725.B55
Bolivia
  History and criticism: ML239.B6, ML3487.B5
  Instruments: ML486.B5
  Vocal music: M1688.B6
Bombardon
  Instruction and study: MT480+
Bombardon music: MT483, MT484
Bones (Musical instrument)
  Instruction and study: MT725.B6
Bongo
  Instruction and study: MT663
Bonkó: ML1038.B66
Bosnia and Hercegovina
  History and criticism: ML263, ML3611.B54
  Vocal music: M1723.3+
Bouzouki
  Instruction and study: MT654.B69
Bowling
  Vocal music: M1977.S715, M1978.S715
Boxing
  Vocal music: M1977.S716, M1978.S716
Boy Scouts of America
  Vocal music: M1977.B6, M1978.B6
Braille music notation: MT38
Brass decets: M957.4
Brass instruments: ML933
  Bibliography: ML128.B73
  Dictionaries: ML102.B7
  Instruction and study: MT418
    For children: MT801.B72
Brass nonets: M957.4
Brass octets: M857.4
Brass quartets: M457.4
Brass quintets: M557.4
Brass septets: M757.4
Brass sextets: M657.4
Brass trios: M357.4
Brazil
  History and criticism: ML232, ML3487.B7
  Instruments: ML486.B7
  Vocal music: M1689+
Brethren Church music
  History and criticism: ML3161
Brethren in Christ Church
  Hymns: M2131.B6
British American folk music
  History and criticism: ML3553
British Americans
  History and criticism: ML3553
  Vocal music: M1668.1
British Isles
  History and criticism: ML285+, ML3650+
  Instruments: ML501
  Vocal music: M1738+
Broadsides: M1628.2+, M1630.3.S69, M1739.3
Bronze drum: ML1038.B7
Brotherhood Week
  Vocal music: M1977.B7, M1978.B7

Buddhism
Rituals: M2188.B8
Buddhist hymns: M2145.B8
Bugle
Instruction and study: MT452
Bugle and drum music: M1270
Bugle and piano music: M270.B8, M271.B8
Bulbultarang
Instruction and study: MT634.B84
Bulgaria
History and criticism: ML252, ML3602
Vocal music: M1712+
Bullfights
Vocal music: M1977.B8, M1978.B8
Button-key accordion
Instruction and study: MT681
Byzantine music
History and criticism: ML188
Byzantine rite: M2160.71+

C

Cadenzas
Collections: M1004.6+
Cajun songs: M1668.8
Calliope music: M175.C3
Camaldolite rite: M2154.4.C34
Camp Fire Girls
Vocal music: M1977.B6, M1978.B6
Campaign songs: M1659.7+
Bibliography: ML128.C13
Campanula: ML927.C36
Instruction and study: MT335.C36
Campanula music: M59.C36
Camping
Vocal music: M1977.C3, M1978.C3
Canada
History and criticism: ML205, ML3484, ML3563
Instruments: ML478
Vocal music: M1678+
Canal Zone
Vocal music: M1672.C2, M1673.C2
Canals
Vocal music: M1977.C34, M1978.C34
Candlemas music
Choruses, etc., Unaccompanied: M2088.C2, M2098.C2
Choruses, etc., with keyboard: M2068.C2, M2078.C2
Liturgy and ritual: M2150.4.C35+
Songs: M2114.8.C2
Canon
Instruction and study: MT59
Cantata: ML2400, ML3260
Cantatas
Analysis, appreciation: MT110+
Bibliography: ML128.C15
Texts: ML53.8+
Cantatas, Sacred
Chorus: M2020+
For children: M2190+
Solo: M2102+
Cantatas, Secular
Chorus: M1629.5
For children: M1996
Solo: M1611+
Cante hondo
History and criticism: ML3712
Canun music
Concertos: M1037.4.C3
Capuchin rite: M2154.4.C36
Car racing
Vocal music: M1978.S707
Carillon music: M172
Carillons: ML1039
Instruction and study: MT710
Carmelite rite: M2154.4.C37
Carols
Dictionaries: ML102.C3
Cars (Automobiles)
Vocal music: M1977.M6, M1978.M6
Castanet music: M175.C35
Castanets
Instruction and study: MT725.C4
Catalogs, Booksellers: ML150
Catches
History and criticism: ML2670
Catholic Church
Ambrosian rite: M2154.6.A45
Armenian rite: M2154.6.A76
Liturgy: M2010+, M2147+
Mozarabic rite: M2154.6.M7
Vocal music: M2069, M2089, M2119
Catholic Church music
History and criticism: ML3002+

Celebrities
Vocal music: M1659.5.A +
Celesta and piano music: M284.C4, M285.C4
Celesta music: M175.C44
Celtic harp: ML1015.C3
Instruction and study: MT552
Celtic harp music: M142.C44
Cemeteries
Vocal music: M1977.C4, M1978.C4
Cenḍa: ML1038.C4
Centennial Exhibition (Philadelphia, 1876)
Vocal music: M1677.2.P4 1876
Central America
History and criticism: ML220 +, ML3487.A +, ML3572
Instruments: ML484
Vocal music: M1684 +
Century of Progress International Exposition (Chicago, 1933)
Vocal music: M1677.2.C3 1933
Chaconne
Instruction and study: MT64.C48
Chalumeau: ML990.C5
Chalumeau music
Concertos: M1034.C5, M1034.5.C5, M1035.C5
Chamber music: M177 +, MT728.2 +
Analysis, appreciation: MT140 +
Bibliography: ML128.C4
Graded lists: ML132.C4
Discography: ML156.4.C4
Early instruments: M990
For children: M1389 +, M1413 +
History and criticism: ML1100 +
Performance: MT728 +
For children: MT810
With voice: M1613.3
Chamber orchestra music: M1000 +
Chance compositions: M1470
Change ringing: MT711
Change ringing (Bells): MT710
Changgo
Instruction and study: MT725.C45
Chants (Plain, Gregorian, etc.)
Dictionaries: ML102.C45
History and criticism: ML3082
Instruction and study: MT860
Charango: ML1015.C37
Instruction and study: MT599.C45
Charts, diagrams, etc.: MT15
Chemistry
Vocal music: M1977.C43, M1978.C43
Cheng: ML1015.C47
Instruction and study: MT654.C47
Cheng music: M142.C49
Chicago International Exposition (1933)
Vocal music: M1677.2.C3 1933
Child musicians: ML81, ML83
Children's Day music: M2191.C4
Children's music: M1990 +, M2190 +
Chile
History and criticism: ML233, ML3487.C55
Instruments: ML486.C5
Vocal music: M1691 +
Chime music: M172
Chimes: ML1039
Instruction and study: MT720
Ch'in: ML1015.C5
Instruction and study: MT654.C5
Chin ch'ien pan
Instruction and study: MT725.C5
Ch'in music: M142.C5
China
History and criticism: ML336, ML3746
Instruments: ML531
Vocal music: M1804 +
Ching hu
Instruction and study: MT335.C5
Ching hu music: M59.C5
Concertos: M1019.C5
Choirs (Musical groups): MT88
Choral music
History and criticism: ML1499 +
Philosophy and aesthetics: ML3873
Choral singing
Instruction and study: M2152, MT875
For children: MT915
Chorale: ML3084, ML3184, ML3265
Chorales
Bibliography: ML128.C46

Cycling
  Vocal music: M1977.S7165, M1978.S7165
Cymbals
  Instruction and study: MT725.C9
Cymbals and piano music: M284.C94, M285.C94
Cyprus
  Vocal music: M1824.C9+, M1825.C9+
Czakan: ML990.C95
  Instruction and study: MT358.C9
Czech Republic
  History and criticism: ML247, ML3590
  Vocal music: M1704+
Czechoslovakia
  History and criticism: ML247, ML3590
  Instruments: ML493
  Vocal music: M1704+

D

Dance band music: M1356+
  Performance: MT733.7
Dance instruction music: M1450
Dance music
  Band: M1247.9+, M1262+
  Bibliography: ML128.D3
  Discography: ML156.4.D3
  History and criticism: ML3400+
  Orchestra: M1047+
  Piano: M30+
  String orchestra: M1147+
  Unspecified instrument(s): M1450
Dance orchestra music: M1350+, M1356+
  History and criticism: ML3518
  Performance: MT733.7
Darabukka
  Instruction and study: MT725.D37
Daughters of the American Revolution
  Vocal music: M1676.D3
Daughters of Union Veterans of the Civil War
  Vocal music: M1676.D4
Daughters of Utah Pioneers
  Vocal music: M1676.D45
Death Valley '49ers
  Vocal music: M1676.D5
Decets
  Instrumental music: M900+
Dedications (Events)
  Music: M1677.3.A+, M2150.3.D42+
Democracy
  Vocal music: M1977.D4, M1978.D4
Democratic Party (U.S.)
  Vocal music: M1662+
DeMolay for Boys
  Vocal music: M1900.M41, M1901.M41
Denmark
  History and criticism: ML311, ML3702
  Instruments: ML514
  Vocal music: M1770+
Descants: M2115.5
Deutscher Orden der Harugari
  Vocal music: M1905.D5, M1906.D5
Dhimay: ML1038.D5
Diction: MT883
Dictionaries: ML100+
Didjeridu: ML990.D53
  Instruction and study: MT533.D53
Directories: ML12+
Disabled American Veterans
  Vocal music: M1676.D6
Discalced Trinitarian rite: M2154.4.D63
Disciples of Christ
  Hymns: M2131.D4
Disco music
  History and criticism: ML3526
Discography: ML156+
  Bibliography: ML128.D56
Divine Science Church (U.S.)
  Hymns: M2131.D5
Dixie (Song): M1630.3.D4
Dobro
  Instruction and study: MT599.D6
Dobro music: M142.D55
Dömbra
  Bibliography: ML128.D58
  Instruction and study: MT643
Dömbra and piano music: M282.D64, M283.D64
Dömbra music: M142.D6
  Concertos: M1037.4.D64
Dominican rite: M2154.4.D65

Doo-wop music
  History and criticism: ML3527
Double bass: ML920+
  Bibliography: ML128.D6
  Instruction and study: MT320+
    For children: MT801.D65
Double bass and piano music: M237+
  For children: M1400
Double bass music: M55+, MT333, MT333.4
  Concertos: M1018, M1118
  For children: M1385.D6
  History and criticism: ML925
Double keyboard music: M25.2, M38.2
Dramatic music: M1500+
  Philosophy and aesthetics: ML3857+
Drinking songs: M1977.D7, M1978.D7
Drum: ML1035+
  Instruction and study: MT662
    For children: MT801.D7
Drum and bugle corps: MT735
Drum and piano music: M284.D8, M285.D8
Drum machine
  Instruction and study: MT724.5
Drum majoring: MT733.5
Drum music: M146
  For children: M1385.D7
Drum set: ML1035+
  Instruction and study: MT662
Drum set music: M146
Duets
  Instrumental music: M180+
  Vocal music: M1529.2+
Dulcimer: ML1041
  Dictionaries: ML102.D85
  Instruction and study: MT717
Dulcimer and piano music: M284.D85, M285.D85
Dulcimer music: M175.D84
  Concertos: M1039.4.D85
Dulcimer, Appalachian, music: M142.A7
Dulzaina: ML990.D8
Dutch American folk music
  History and criticism: ML3555
Dutch Reformed Church
  Hymns: M2124.D7
  Liturgy and ritual: M2164
Dutch Reformed church music
  History and criticism: ML3164

E

Eagles, Fraternal Order of
  Vocal music: M1905.E2, M1906.E2
Early instruments
  Chamber music: M990
Easter music
  Choruses, etc., with keyboard: M2066, M2076
  Choruses, Unaccompanied: M2086, M2096
  For children: M2191.E2
  Liturgy and ritual: M2148.3.E2, M2149.4.E25, M2149.5.V54
  Organ: M14.4.E2, M14.5.E2
  Songs, etc.: M1629.3.E3, M2114.6
Eastern Star, Order of
  Vocal music: M1905.E3, M1906.E3
Ecology
  Vocal music: M1977.C53, M1978.C53
Economic conditions
  Vocal music: M1977.E3, M1978.E3
Ecuador
  History and criticism: ML235, ML3487.E2
  Instruments: ML486.E25
  Vocal music: M1687.E2, M1688.E2
Education
  Vocal music: M1977.E33, M1978.E33
El Salvador
  History and criticism: ML227
  Vocal music: M1684.S2, M1685.S2
Elche, Festa de
  Bibliography: ML128.E38
Election Day
  Vocal music: M1629.3.E5
Electric guitar
  Instruction and study: MT599.E4
Electric guitar music: M142.E4
Electronic composition: MT56
Electronic instrument and piano music: M284.E4, M285.E4
Electronic instrument music
  Concertos: M1039.4.E35
Electronic instruments: ML1091.8+
Electronic keyboard instruments
  Instruction and study: MT192

Electronic music: M1473
Bibliography: ML128.E4
Dictionaries: ML102.E4
Discography: ML156.4.E4
History and criticism: ML1379+
Electronic organ music: M14.8+
Concertos: M1039.4.E37
For children: M1385.E4
Electronic percussion instruments
Instruction and study: MT724.5
Electronium music
Concertos: M1039.4.E4
Elizabeth Sprague Coolidge Foundation: ML29
Elks, Benevolent and Protective Order of
Vocal music: M1905.E5, M1906.E5
Embellishment
Instruction and study: MT80
Emigration and immigration
Vocal music: M1977.E68, M1978.E68
Encyclopedias and dictionaries: ML100+
England
History and criticism: ML286, ML3492, ML3652
Vocal music: M1740+
English guitar music: M142.E5
English horn
Bibliography: ML128.O2
Instruction and study: MT376
English horn and piano music: M270.E5, M271.E5
English horn music: M110.E5
Concertos: M1034.E5, M1034.5.E5, M1035.E5, M1134.E5, M1134.5.E5, M1135.E5
Environmental music
Discography: ML156.4.E5
Epinette des Vosges
Instruction and study: MT654.E6
Epiphany music
Choruses, etc., Unaccompanied: M2088.E5, M2098.E5
Choruses, etc., with keyboard: M2068.E5, M2078.E5
For children: M2191.E6
Liturgy and ritual: M2148.3.E6
Organ: M14.4.E6
Songs: M2114.8.E5
Episcopal Church
Hymns: M2125
Erh hu
Instruction and study: MT335.E7
Erh hu music: M59.E7
Concertos: M1019.E8
Estonia
History and criticism: ML303, ML3681.E8
Instruments: ML508.E8
Vocal music: M1766.E4+, M1767.E6+
Ethics
Vocal music: M1977.M55, M1978.M55
Ethnic music
History and criticism: ML3544+
Ethnic songs: M1668+
Ethnomusicology: ML3797.6+
Bibliography: ML128.E8
Euphonium
Bibliography: ML128.B24
Instruction and study: MT496
Euphonium and piano music: M270.B37, M271.B37
Euphonium music: M110.B33
Concertos: M1034.B37, M1034.5.B37, M1035.B37, M1134.B37, M1134.5.B37, M1135.B37
Europe
History and criticism: ML240+, ML3580+
Instruments: ML489+
Vocal music: M1698+
Evangelical church music
History and criticism: ML3167
Evangelical Mission Covenant Church of America
Hymns: M2131.E8
Ex-convicts
Vocal music: M1977.C55, M1978.C55
Examinations, questions, etc.: MT9
Exhibition catalogs: ML141.A+
Exhibitions
Vocal music: M1677.2.A+
Expo 67 (Montreal, 1967)
Vocal music: M1677.2.M65 1967
Expo 74 (Spokane, 1974)
Vocal music: M1677.2.S65 1974

F

Facsimiles: M2+, ML94.5
  Literature: ML95.5
  Music: ML96.4+
Famous people
  Vocal music: M1627.5.A+, M1659.A+, M1659.5.A+
Farmer-Labor Party
  Vocal music: M1664.F15, M1665.F15
Farmers
  Vocal music: M1977.F2, M1978.F2
Farmers' Alliance (U.S.)
  Vocal music: M1664.F2, M1665.F2
Fathers
  Vocal music: M1977.F26, M1978.F26
Father's Day music
  Choruses, etc., Unaccompanied: M2088.F3, M2098.F3
  Choruses, etc., with keyboard: M2068.F3, M2078.F3
  For children: M2191.F38
  Songs: M2114.8.F3
Faust, d. ca. 1540: ML2100
  Discography: ML156.4.F35
Federal Party (U.S.)
  Vocal music: M1664.F4, M1665.F4
Festivals: ML35+, ML3544.5
Festschriften: ML55
Field music: M1270
  Performance: MT735
Fife
  Instruction and study: MT356
Fife and drum corps: MT735
Fife and drum music: M1270
Fife music: M110.F43
Filipino Federation of America
  Vocal music: M1676.F5
Finland
  History and criticism: ML269, ML3619
  Vocal music: M1729.3+
Fire fighters
  Vocal music: M1977.F4, M1978.F4
Fire prevention
  Vocal music: M1977.F38, M1978.F38
Fishers
  Vocal music: M1977.F5, M1978.F5
Flag Day
  Vocal music: M1629.3.F4
Flageolet
  Instruction and study: MT359
    For children: MT801.F4
Flageolet music: M110.F5
Flamenco
  Dictionaries: ML102.F55
Flamenco music
  History and criticism: ML3712
Flaviol: ML990.F6
Flaviol music: M110.F52
Flowers
  Vocal music: M1977.F54, M1978.F
Flügelhorn
  Instruction and study: MT493
Flügelhorn and piano music: M270.F7, M271.F7
Flügelhorn music: M110.F53
  Concertos: M1034.F6, M1034.5.F6, M1035.F6, M1134.F7, M1134.5.F7, M1135.F7
Flute: ML935+
  Bibliography: ML128.F7
  Instruction and study: MT340+
    For children: MT801.F5
Flute and piano music: M240+
Flute music: M60+, MT343, MT344
  Concertos: M1020+, M1120+
  For children: M1385.F6
  History and criticism: ML937
Flutophone
  Instruction and study
    For children: MT801.T6
Folk dance music
  Discography: ML156.4.F45
Folk music
  Bibliography: ML128.F74
  Dictionaries: ML102.F66
  Discography: ML156.4.F5
  History and criticism: ML3544+
Folk songs: M1627+
  Bibliography: ML128.F75
  Discography: ML156.4.F6
Football
  Vocal music: M1977.S718, M1978.S
Forest fires
  Vocal music: M1977.F6, M1978.F6
Foresters and forestry
  Vocal music: M1977.F6, M1978.F6
Foresters societies
  Vocal music: M1905.W7, M1906.W
Forty and Eight
  Vocal music: M1676.Q3

Horn music: M80+, MT423, MT424
Concertos: M1028+, M1128+
Discography: ML156.4.H7
For children: M1385.H6
History and criticism: ML958
Horse racing
Vocal music: M1977.S723, M1978.S723
Horsemanship
Vocal music: M1977.S722, M1978.S722
House music
History and criticism: ML3528.5
Housewives
Vocal music: M1977.H65, M1978.H65
Hsiao: ML990.H75
Instruction and study: MT358.H7
Hsiao music: M110.H7
Hu hu
Instruction and study: MT335.H83
Humor: ML65
Humorous songs: M1977.H7, M1978.H7
Hungary
History and criticism: ML248, ML3593
Instruments: ML494
Vocal music: M1706+
Hunger
Vocal music: M1977.H77, M1978.H77
Hunting songs: M1977.H8, M1978.H8
History and criticism: ML3780
Hurdy-gurdy: ML1086
Instruction and study: MT725.H87
Hurdy-gurdy music: M175.H9
Concertos: M1039.4.H87
Husbands
Vocal music: M1977.H85, M1978.H85
Hutterian Brethren
Hymns: M2131.H87
Hymnals: M2115+
Hindu: M2145.H55
Sikh: M2145.S57
Hymnology: ML3186, ML3270
Hymns: M2115+
Bibliography: ML128.H8
Dictionaries: ML102.H95
History and criticism: ML3086
Hyŏn' gŭm music: M142.H9

I

I AM religious activity
Hymns: M2131.I2
Iceland
History and criticism: ML314
Vocal music: M1771.3+
Ichigenkin: ML1015.I3
Ichigenkin music: M142.I3
Iconography
Catalogs: ML140
Ideal harp
Instruction and study: MT634.I3
Immigration
Vocal music: M1977.E68, M1978.E68
Implements, utensils, etc. as instruments
Instruction and study: MT722
Improvisation (Music)
History: ML430.7
Instruction and study: MT68, MT191.I5, MT239
Incidental music: M1510+
Bibliography: ML128.I6
History and criticism: ML2000
Philosophy and aesthetics: ML3860
Independence Day (U.S.)
Vocal music: M1629.3.F5
India
History and criticism: ML338, ML3748
Instruments: ML533
Vocal music: M1808+
Indian Ocean islands
Vocal music: M1846
Indians of North America
History and criticism: ML3557
Music
Discography: ML156.4.I5
Vocal music: M1669
Industrial Workers of the World
Vocal music: M1664.L3, M1665.L3
Institutions: ML32+
Instruction and study: MT1+
Audio-visual aids: MT150
Examinations, questions, etc.: MT9
For children: MT740+

J

Koto music: M142.K6
  Concertos: M1037.4.K68
Kotsuzumi: ML1038.K7
Ku-Klux Klan
  Vocal music: M1664.K7, M1665.K7
Kuan music: M110.K8
  Concertos: M1034.K8, M1034.5.K8, M1035.K8
Kyriales: M2148.4.A+

L

Labor
  Vocal music: M1977.L3, M1978.L3
    History and criticism: ML3780
Labor Day
  Vocal music: M1629.3.L3
Labor songs
  Discography: ML156.4.L2
Ländler
  Instruction and study: MT64.L23
Latin America
  History and criticism: ML199, ML3487.A+, ML3558
Latvia
  History and criticism: ML304, ML3681.L4
  Instruments: ML508.L4
  Vocal music: M1758+
Lead sheets: M1356.2
Left hand piano music: M26
Lenten music
  Bibliography: ML128.L2
  Choruses, etc., Unaccompanied: M2088.L5, M2098.L5
  Choruses, etc., with keyboard: M2068.L5, M2078.L5
  For children: M2191.L5
  Liturgy and ritual: M2148.3.P3
  Organ: M14.4.L5, M14.5.L5
  Songs: M2114.8.L5
Liber usualis: M2151.A+
Librettists
  Biography: ML403, ML423.A+
Libretto: ML2110
Librettos: ML47+
  Bibliography: ML128.L5
Liechtenstein
  History and criticism: ML325.L5
  Vocal music: M1788.L76+
Lincoln's Birthday
  Vocal music: M1629.3.L5
Liquimofono: ML990.L57
Lira da braccio: ML927.L57
Literature on music: ML1+
Lithuania
  History and criticism: ML305, ML3681.L6
  Instruments: ML508.L6
  Vocal music: M1766.L4+, M1767.L4+
Littering
  Vocal music: M1977.L55, M1978.L55
Liu ch'in
  Instruction and study: MT654.L58
Lo ku
  Instruction and study: MT725.L6
Logier, Johann Bernhard, d. 1846
  Method of musical composition: MT24
Louisiana Purchase Exposition (St. Louis, 1904)
  Vocal music: M1677.2.S25 1904
Lumbermen
  Vocal music: M1977.L8, M1978.L8
Lur music: M110.L9
Lute: ML1010+
  Bibliography: ML128.L88
  Instruction and study: MT640
Lute and piano music: M282.L88, M283.L88
Lute music: M140+
  Concertos: M1137.4.L88
  History: ML1012+
Lutheran Church
  Hymns: M2126
  Liturgy and ritual: M2017, M2172+
Lutheran church music
  History and criticism: ML3168
Luxembourg
  Vocal music: M1788.L8+
Lyceum League
  Vocal music: M1676.L97
Lyra: ML927.L9
Lyra viol: ML927.L97
Lyra viol music: M59.L9
Lyre: ML1015.L89
  Instruction and study: MT644
Lyre-guitar: ML1015.L9

M

Macedonia (Republic)
  History and criticism: ML264, ML3611.M3
  Vocal music: M1725.3+
Madrigals
  Bibliography: ML128.M2
Mail carriers
  Vocal music: M1977.M3, M1978.M3
Malta
  History and criticism: ML325.M3
  Vocal music: M1788.M3+
Managers
  Biography: ML406, ML429.A+
Mandola
  Instruction and study: MT611
Mandola music: M142.M25
Mandolin: ML1015.M2
  Bibliography: ML128.M23
  Instruction and study: MT600+
    For children: MT801.M3
Mandolin and piano music: M278+
Mandolin guitar
  Instruction and study: MT634.M35
Mandolin harp music: M175.M3
Mandolin music: M130+, MT603, MT608.5
  Concertos: M1037.4.M3, M1137.4.M3
Mandolin orchestra music: M1360
  Performance: MT734
Mandoloncello
  Instruction and study: MT612
Manuscripts: M1490, M2147, M2156, ML93+
  Classification: M1+
  Facsimiles: M2+, M2147, M2156, ML93+, ML95.5, ML96.4+
Maracas
  Instruction and study: MT725.M4
Marches
  Band: M1247, M1260
  Bibliography: ML128.M25
  Orchestra: M1046
  String orchestra: M1146
Marching band routines: M1269
Marching bands: MT733.4
Marimba: ML1048
  Instruction and study: MT719
    For children: MT801.X9
Marimba and piano music: M284.X9, M285.X9
Marimba music: M175.X6
  For children: M1385.X9
Marseillaise
  History and criticism: ML3621.M37
Mary, Blessed Virgin, Saint
  Choruses, etc., Unaccompanied: M2088.M33, M2098.M33
  Choruses, etc., with keyboard: M2068.M33, M2078.M33
  Masses: M2148.3.A88, M2148.3.B59, M2148.3.I46, M2148.3.M3
  Offices: M2149.5.L52, M2149.5.V55
  Songs: M2114.8.M33
Masques with music: M1520+
Mass (Music): ML3088
Masses (Music): M2010+
  For children: M2190+
Maundy Thursday music
  Choruses, etc., Unaccompanied: M2088.M35, M2098.M35
  Choruses, etc., with keyboard: M2068.M35, M2078.M35
  Liturgy and ritual: M2148.3.H64, M2149.4.H69
  Songs: M2114.8.M35
Mauritius
  Vocal music: M1846.M4+
May Day
  Vocal music: M1977.M37, M1978.M
Mazdaznan hymns: M2131.M2
Mbira: ML1015.M25
  Instruction and study: MT654.M38
Mbira music: M142.M3
Mechanical musical instrument music: M174.A+
Mechanical musical instruments: ML1049.8+
Mechanical organ: ML1058
Medical apects of music
  Bibliography: ML128.M27
Medicine
  Vocal music: M1977.M4, M1978.M4
Meistersinger: ML183
Mellophone and piano music: M270.M4, M271.M4
Melodeon music: M175.M38
Melodica: ML1089.M45
  Instruction and study: MT533.M4

Morin khuur
  Instruction and study:
    MT335.M67
Mormon Church
  Hymns: M2129
  Liturgy and ritual: M2179
Mormon church music
  History and criticism: ML3174
Motets
  Bibliography: ML128.M67
Mothers
  Vocal music: M1977.M57, M1978.M57
Mother's Day
  Choruses, etc., Unaccompanied:
    M2088.M6, M2098.M6
  Choruses, etc., with keyboard:
    M2068.M6, M2078.M6
  Songs: M2114.8.M6
  Vocal music
    For children: M2191.M6
Motion picture music: M176, M1527+
  Bibliography: ML128.M7
  Dictionaries: ML102.M68
  Discography: ML156.4.M6
  History and criticism: ML2074+
  Instruction and study: MT64.M65
Mountaineering
  Vocal music: M1977.M63, M1978.M63
Mouth organs: ML1088+
  Instruction and study: MT682+
Mozarabic rite: M2154.6.M7
Mridanga: ML1038.M74
  Instruction and study: MT725.M7
Musette
  Instruction and study: MT373
Music
  500-1400
    Bibliography: ML128.M3
  Acoustics and physics: ML3805+
  Analysis, appreciation: MT90+
    Bibliography: ML128.A7
  Anecdotes: ML65
  Awards: ML75.5+
    Bibliography: ML128.P68
  Bibliography: ML112.8+
    Graded lists: ML132.A+
  Competitions: ML75.5+
    Bibliography: ML128.P68
  Computer network resources:
    ML74.7
Music
  Dictionaries: ML100+
    Pronunciation: ML109
  Discography: ML156+
  Encyclopedias: ML100+
  Exhibition catalogs: ML141.A+
  For children: M1990+, M2190+
    Bibliography: ML128.J8
    Discography: ML156.4.C5
  History and criticism: ML55+,
    ML159+
    Juvenile literature: ML3928+
  Humor: ML65
  Instruction and study: MT1+
    Bibliography: ML128.I64
  Manuscripts: ML93+
    Bibliography: ML135
    Facsimiles: ML93+
  Medical apects
    Bibliography: ML128.M27
  Philosophy and aesthetics:
    ML3845+
  Physiological aspects: ML3820+
    Bibliography: ML128.M27
  Pictorial works: ML89
    Catalogs: ML140
  Psychological aspects: ML3830+
  Publishing: ML112+
    Vocal music: M1977.M8, M1978.M8
  Scores
    Bibliography: ML128.S29
  Software: ML74.3+
  Terminology: ML108
  Theory: MT5.5+
    Bibliography: ML128.T5
  Vocational guidance: ML70+
Music and literature: ML79+
Music and society: ML3795
Music and war
  Bibliography: ML128.W2
Music appreciation: MT90+
  Bibliography: ML128.A7
Music box: ML1065+
Music box music: M174.M85
Music by women composers
  Discography: ML156.4.W6
Music copying: MT35
Music critics
  Biography: ML403, ML423.A+
Music dealers
  Biography: ML405, ML427.A+

N

Nikolaus, von der Flüe, Saint, 1417-1487
  Songs
    History and criticism: ML3722.N54
Nonets
  Instrumental music: M900+
North America
  History and criticism: ML200+
  Vocal music: M1680+
North Korea
  History and criticism: ML343, ML3753
  Vocal music: M1818+
Northern Ireland
  History and criticism: ML3492
  Vocal music: M1745.3+
Norway
  History and criticism: ML312, ML3704
  Instruments: ML515
  Vocal music: M1772+
Notation
  History: ML431+
  Instruction and study: MT35+
Nurses
  Vocal music: M1977.N8, M1978.N8
Nutrition
  Vocal music: M1977.N83, M1978.N83

O

Oboe: ML940+
  Bibliography: ML128.O2
  Instruction and study: MT360+
Oboe and piano music: M245+
Oboe d'amore
  Bibliography: ML128.O2
Oboe d'amore and piano music: M270.O26, M271.O26
Oboe d'amore music
  Concertos: M1034.O26, M1034.5.O26, M1035.O26, M1134.O26, M1134.5.O26, M1135.O26
Oboe music: M65+, MT363, MT364
  Concertos: M1022+, M1122+
  History and criticism: ML943
Oboette
  Instruction and study: MT372
Ocarina: ML990.O3
  Instruction and study: MT526
Ocarina and piano music: M270.O3, M271.O3
Ocarina music: M110.O3
Oceania
  History and criticism: ML360, ML3770
  Instruments: ML547
Octets
  Instrumental music: M800+
Odd-Fellows, Independent Order of
  Vocal music: M1905.O3, M1906.O3
Odes
  History and criticism: ML2400
Old Catholic Church
  Liturgy and ritual: M2155.5
Old Folks Concert Troupe: M1677
Olympics
  Vocal music: M1977.O5, M1978.O5
Ondes Martenot
  Instruction and study: MT724
Ondes Martenot and piano music: M284.O5, M285.O5
Ondes Martenot music: M175.O5
  Concertos: M1039.4.O5, M1139.4.O5
Ongnyugŭm
  Instruction and study: MT634.O58
Opera: ML1699+
  Dictionaries: ML102.O6
  Instruction and study: MT64.O6
  Philosophy and aesthetics: ML3858
Opera plots: MT95+
Operas: M1500+
  Bibliography: ML128.O4
  China: M1805.3+
  Discography: ML156.4.O46
  Film catalogs: ML158.6.O6
  For children: M1995
  Korea (North): M1819.3
  Librettos: ML48+, ML52.65+, ML52.75+
  Performance: MT955+
  Stories, plots, etc.: MT95+
  Video catalogs: ML158.6.O6
  Vocal scores with piano: M1503
Operatic scenes: M1509
Operetta: ML1900
Operettas: M1500+
Ophicleide: ML990.O7
  Instruction and study: MT520

PTA
  Vocal music: M1920.P2, M1921.P2
Puerto Rico
  History and criticism: ML207.P8
  Vocal music: M1681.P6+
Pung: ML1038.P85
  Instruction and study: MT725.P8

Q

Quaker church music
  History and criticism: ML3167.5
Quartets
  Instrumental music: M400+
  Vocal music: M1529.4+
Quebec liturgy (Catholic): M2154.2.Q4
Quena: ML990.Q46
  Instruction and study: MT358.Q4
Quintets
  Instrumental music: M500+
  Vocal music: M1529.4+

R

Rabāb: ML927.R33
Radio
  Vocal music: M1977.R2, M1978.R2
Radio and music: ML68
Radio music: M176.5, M1527.5+
Raga
  Bibliography: ML128.R25
  Dictionaries: ML102.R2
Ragtime music
  Discography: ML156.4.R25
  History and criticism: ML3530
Railroad Fair (Chicago, 1948)
  Vocal music: M1677.2.C3 1948
Railroads
  Vocal music: M1977.R3, M1978.R3
Rainbow, Order of, for Girls
  Vocal music: M1905.R3, M1906.R3
Rally Day music
  For children: M2191.R2
Rap music
  Bibliography: ML128.R28
  History and criticism: ML3531
Readings with music: M1625+
Rebana: ML1038.R43
Rebekah Assemblies, International Association of, IOOF
  Vocal music: M1905.R33, M1906.R33
Recitations with music: M1625+
  With sacred chorus: M2020.3, M2023.3
  With secular chorus: M1530.3, M1533.3, M1538.3, M1540.3, M1543.3, M1544.3
Recorder: ML990.R4
  Bibliography: ML128.R31
  Instruction and study: MT350+
    For children: MT801.R4
Recorder and piano music: M270.R4, M271.R4
Recorder music: M110.R4, MT352.5, MT352.6
  Concertos: M1034.R4, M1034.5.R4, M1035.R4, M1134.R4, M1134.5.R4, M1135.R4
  Discography: ML156.4.R34
  For children: M1385.R3
Reed organ: ML597
  Instruction and study: MT200+
Reed organ music: M15+
  For children: M1375
  History and criticism: ML649
Reed organ music (2 reed organs): M190
Reformation Festival music
  Choruses, etc., Unaccompanied: M2088.R3, M2098.R3
  Choruses, etc., with keyboard: M2068.R3, M2078.R3
  Songs: M2114.8.R3
Reformed Church
  Hymns: M2124.A+
  Liturgy and ritual: M2164
Reggae music
  Discography: ML156.4.R36
  History and criticism: ML3532
Republican Party (U.S. : 1854-)
  Vocal music: M1660+
Requiems: M2010+, M2148.3.D4
  History and criticism: ML3088
Research: ML3797+
Revivals
  Vocal music: M2198+
Revolutionary songs
  History and criticism: ML3621.R48

T

U

United Church of Religious
  Science
  Hymns: M2131.U63
United Daughters of the
  Confederacy
  Vocal music: M1676.U7
United Nations
  Children's Fund
    Vocal music: M1920.U48, M1921.U48
United Service Organizations
  (U.S.) (USO)
  Vocal music: M1676.U77
United States
  Cities
    Vocal music: M1657+
  History and criticism: ML200,
      ML3476.8+, ML3551+
  Imprints: M1.A1+, M20.C58+
  Instruments: ML476
  National Recovery
    Administration
    Vocal music: M1665.N3
  Relations with Mexico, 1914-
    1917
    Vocal music: M1645
  States
    Vocal music: M1629.7.A+, M1657+
  Vocal music: M1628+
Unity School of Christianity
  Hymns: M2131.U65
Universalist Church
  Hymns: M2131.U7
Unspecified instrument and
  piano music: M285.5+
Unspecified instrument music:
    M59.5, M111, M175.5
  Concertos: M1139.5
  Duets: M298.5
  For children: M1385.M3
Ursuline rite: M2154.4.U8
Uruguay
  History and criticism: ML237,
      ML3487.U8
  Vocal music: M1687.U6, M1688.U6
Utensils, etc., as musical
  instruments
  Instruction and study: MT722

V

Valiha
  Instruction and study:
    MT634.V35
Vaudeville songs: M1622
Venezuela
  History and criticism: ML238,
      ML3487.V4
  Instruments: ML486.V45
  Vocal music: M1687.V3, M1688.V3
Vespers (Music): M2149.2.V4,
    M2149.5.V5+
Veterans Day
  Vocal music: M1629.3.V4
Veterans of Foreign Wars of the
  United States
  Ladies' Auxiliary
    Vocal music: M1676.V4+
  Vocal music: M1676.V4+
Vibraharp music: M175.X6
  For children: M1385.X9
Vibraphone: ML1048
  Instruction and study: MT719
    For children: MT801.X9
Vibraphone and piano music:
    M284.X9, M285.X9
Vibraphone music: M175.X6
  For children: M1385.X9
Video recordings
  Catalogs: ML158.4+
Vietnamese Conflict, 1961-1975
  Vocal music: M1650
Vihuela music: M142.V53
Vina: ML1015.V5
  Instruction and study:
    MT654.V56
Vina music: M142.V55
Viol: ML927.V5
  Bibliography: ML128.V35
Viol music: M59.V53
Viola: ML900+
  Bibliography: ML128.V36
  Instruction and study: MT280+
    For children: MT760+
Viola and piano music: M224+
  For children: M1393+
Viola da braccio
  Instruction and study: MT338
Viola da gamba
  Instruction and study: MT337

X

Y

Z